Residential Building Inspector

By Cliff Burger

**Study Guide and Practice Questions Workbook for the
ICC® Residential Building Inspector Certification Exam, B1**
Based on the 2012 ICC Residential Building Code

**Visit us at: www.bgrtech.com for the latest version of all the Work Study
Guides**

ISBN₁₀: 0-9792191-2-4

ISBN₁₃: 978-0-9792191-2-2

Printed in USA

IMPORTANT NOTICES AND DISCLAIMERS CONCERNING THIS BOOK

NOTICE AND DISCLAIMER OF LIABILITY CONCERNING THE USE OF THESE DOCUMENTS

Every effort has been made to produce an accurate study aid with the sole goal of helping professionals prepare for the Inspection Exam.

The codes, standards, recommended practices, and guides, of which this document is base on is the ICC® 2012 Residential Building Code®.

IBC®, ICC®, and International Building Code® are all registered trademarks and the property of the International Code Council®. Burger, Inc. does not claim to have nor does it have any affiliation with ICC® or. Portions of the content of this document have been reproduced from 2012 International Residential Code, Copyright 2012. Washington, DC: with permission from the International Code Council®, All rights reserved.

Burger, Inc disclaims liability for any personal injury, property or other damages of any nature whatsoever, whether, special, indirect, consequential or compensatory, directly or indirectly resulting from the publication, use of, or reliance on this document. Burger, Inc makes no guaranty or warranty as to the accuracy or completeness of any information published herein.

This document shall be used solely for the purpose of preparation for the ICC® Inspector Exam. This Document should not be used for any other purpose. You must use the IRC® for any code related need. By making this document available, Burger, Inc. is not undertaking to render professional or other services for or on behalf of any person or entity. Nor is Burger, Inc undertaking to perform any duty owed by any person or entity to someone else. Anyone using this document should rely on his or her own independent judgment or, as appropriate, seek the advice of a competent professional in determining the exercise of reasonable care in any given circumstances.

Residential Building Inspector Practice Exam Questions
384 Unique Questions

There are 60 questions on the B-1 Exam.

That is equivalent to taking the exam over **6 times!!**

The Result: Passed

All Questions are based on the ICC Residential Building Code 2012

by Cliff Burger, ICC Certifications: B-1, E-1, M-1, P-1, B-2 Other: CompTIA A+, Network+, 30 years in the Construction Industry as a Building Contractor, Master Electrician, Electrical Contractor and Businessman.

The best way to study for an open book test is by doing open book tests. By reading a question and then pursuing the answer your mind is forced to interpret what you read, process that information, and find a solution through recall, and research. These study exam questions will help you by improving your skill of three major things needed to pass the exam:

1. You will increase your speed at finding the answers and you will become an expert on where to find the answers in the code book, this is very important because this is the only way to be correct 100% of the time.

2. You will learn the answers to many of the questions that will be on the test and thereby be able to answer them from **recall** memory, saving you precious time.

3. You will become an expert at managing that time during the test, through test taking experience.

The Test Questions Answers and References are in back of the book.

You can **Pass** all the exams first try with these study questions!

Good Luck!

How to Pass Your Exams First Time, Every Time

Studying the code can help you pass the exam, but because of the extremely large amount of data, exceptions and variations it is impossible to have all that information flawlessly in your mind. That is why the tests are open book. The best inspectors rely on the code book, not their recollection of the code. It is extremely important to be *right* on the safety issues in the code. If you have a basic understanding of terminology you should easily be able to pass the exams by having a fast system down for finding the answers in the book.

First, do not read the code through intensely paying attention to every detail. There is way too much information to absorb in that way. Instead, first skim through the table of contents to see how the code is arranged. In an open book test it is very important to be able to find the answer and find it fast. Spend 10 minutes and just familiarize yourself with the arrangement of the whole code book. Look though the table of contents. Go to the sections that interest you and find them. Next, go to the back of the book and study the index. Most of the answers you need to find are only seconds away once you find the right topic in the index. You must become an expert at finding what you need in the index. The answers to almost all of the questions on the exam can be found in a matter of a minute or less if you find it first in the index and then in the section that the index points to.

Second, skim through all of the sections in the code paying attention to the titles of each section and subsection lightly skimming the content. This does two things. It further familiarizes you with the code book and how it is arranged and also trains your eyes and mind to be able to go quickly through the content. You will pick up bits and pieces of what you have skimmed and when you see numbers your mind will naturally be inquisitive to see what the numbers apply to.

Let's face it, on an open book test the main thing to overcome is the time factor. All of the answers that you need are right there in that book, you just need to know where and how to find them. If there were no time limit everyone should be able to get 100% correct answers on the test every time.

How to Learn
One thing that they do not teach you in school is *how to learn and how to remember.* Too much emphasis is put on what you are learning and no emphasis is put on a system of learning.

Schools should first teach you how to learn, just like they teach you how to read or do math. Once you have mastered the system of how to learn, you can learn and retain anything.

Most people think that in order to memorize something you need to read it over and over again. While this method will cause memorization over time, it is really an inefficient use of time.

In reality memorization is a product of two things, time and recall. If you read a fact or figure and then never make any attempt to bring that information back to your conscious mind, you probably will not remember it very long. Think about how many people you have meet only to forget their name. Why because you did not use their name. Remember, if you don't use it, you lose it. Sound familiar, well, it's true.

So I'm learning codes, how do I use them?

Here is how to do it!

Never spend more than about 20 minutes at one time studying through the code book. Why? It is a proven fact that most people concentrate the best for about 20 minutes and then their learning productivity starts to decrease. You will actually learn much more by studying in twenty minute intervals. During the break times away from the code book you will actually keep learning and really learning it if you do this. Try to recall as many of the facts that you have learned during your 20 minute study block as you can. Every time you recall a fact it makes that fact much easier to recall the next time.

The secret is recall over time though not just recall. If you take in any bit of information an within 20 minutes recall that information, then recall it again this time say 3 hours later. You are apt to remember it tomorrow, so if you recall it tomorrow, you are apt to remember it a week from now. Now if you recall it a week from now you will then be able to recall it a month and then a year and the 10 years or for life.

Look at what you did. You read something once, remembered it 6 or 7 times, and now it is imbedded in your memory for life. It actually was imbedded in your mind, the first time you read it. You just needed to then, train your mind how to find it up there in that mass of gray matter.

The first recall is the most important, because if you wait to long your mind my not find the path to the information. Then you have to look it up again and start over. You will learn from experience how long to wait between learning and recalls, 1,2,3,4, 5 ......

So through recall over time you have trained your mind where to find the information that it stores. This simple technique will work for anything you ever need to learn for the rest of your life. The same exact principles can be used on the code book.

Section One in the Book.

Now that you have a good foundation on how to learn and have reviewed the table of contents, the index and skimmed the whole book once, you are ready to start using the practice questions in section one. Use the same twenty minute period method to answer the first practice questions in the workbook. You will probably be able to find from 3 to 6 answers at first in that twenty minute block, and that will keep improving as you practice your skills.   Now use the recall technique between each block, reviewing the questions and answers in your mind. You can be watching TV, eating going for a walk, bike riding playing with the kids, visiting with friends, or doing nearly anything during this time, actually diversion and distractions are a good thing when it comes to recall. If you can recall under those conditions, think how easy it would be on a test with no distractions. Who knew learning could be this much fun?

Going in 20 minute blocks using recall go through all of the practice questions. Remember to think about questions and answers that you did in the last 20 minute block. By the time you are done with the main question area in the book, you will be pretty good at finding answers in the code book, and you will have memorized the answers to many of the questions on the exam. Remember, If you can answer them from memory, accurately you save more time for the ones that you have to look up in the book.

The Second Section, Timed Exams

The timed exams will reinforce all of the skills that you are developing and prepare you for the against the clock aspect of the test. The whole time you are building skills in finding answers, memorizing answers through recall and building confidence. By test day you have become a pro at taking the tests and probably know about one third or more of the answers on the test without even looking them up. And, as for the one's you need to look up, you are very good at finding those answers quickly by now.

Enough said, you are ready to start your first 20 minute block, and happy learning.

ICC Residential Building Inspector EXAM ID: B1 Certification Exam Outline

- 60 multiple-choice questions
- 2-hour time limit
- Open book

The Reference for this Exam and Workbook is:

2012 ICC International Residential Code

B1 Residential Building Inspector			60 multiple-choice questions
			Exam fee: $110 (P&P); $160 (CBT)
			Open book—2-hour time limit
Content Area	% of Total		Reference
Code Administration	4%		2009 *International Residential Code*®
Building Planning	8%		
Footings and Foundations	16%		
Floor Construction	14%		
Wall Construction and Coverings	27%		
Roof/Ceiling Construction and Penetrations	14%		
Public Safety	17%		
Total	100%		

Section 1

384 Practice Questions

1.   The minimum width for concrete and masonry footings for a 3 story conventional light frame construction dwelling where the soil load bearing value is 5000 psf is _____ inches.

    A. 12
    B. 15
    C. 17
    D. 29

2.   Additions, alterations or repairs to any structure shall conform to that required for a new structure _____ the existing structure to comply with all of the requirements of this code, unless otherwise stated.

    A. shall require
    B. must require
    C. without requiring
    D. none of the above

3.   Emergency escape and rescue openings shall have a minimum net clear opening of _____ on grade floor openings.

    A. 7.5
    B. 5.7
    C. 5
    D. 9

4.   A porous layer of gravel, crushed stone or coarse sand shall be placed to a minimum thickness of _____ inches under the basement floor. Provision shall be made for automatic draining of this layer and the gravel or crushed stone wall footings.

    A. 2
    B. 3
    C. 4
    D. 6

5.   Handrails on a ramp adjacent to a wall shall have a space of not less than _____inches between the wall and the handrails.

A. 2
B. 2.5
C. 1.75
D. 1.5

6.   Additions, alterations or repairs shall not cause a(n)
_____ to become unsafe or adversely affect the performance
of the building.

    A. existing structure
    B. new structure
    C. temporary
    D. none of the above

7.   The finished grade of under floor surface may be located at the bottom
of the footings, where there is evidence that the groundwater table can rise to
within _____ inches of the finished floor at the building perimeter or where there
is evidence that the surface water does not readily drain from the building site,
the grade in the under floor space shall be as high as the outside finished
grade, unless an approved drainage system is provided.

    A. 4
    B. 6
    C. 8
    D. 12

8.   The construction documents submitted with the application for permit
shall be accompanied by a _____ showing the size and location of new
construction and existing structures on the site and distances from lot lines.

    A. layout sketch
    B. plot rendering
    C. site plan
    D. none of these

9.   Openings for required guards on the sides of stair treads shall not allow
a sphere _____ inches to pass through.

A. 4
B. 4 3/8
C. 6
D. 6 3/8

10. A stair nosing is not required where the tread depth is a minimum of _____ inches.

    A. 10
    B. 11
    C. 12
    D. 11.5

11. Concrete slab-on-ground floors shall be a minimum _____ inches thick.

    A. 4.5
    B. 4
    C. 3
    D. 3.5

12. The greatest stair nosing projection shall not exceed the smallest nosing projection by more than _____ inch between two stories, including the nosing at the level of floors and landings.

    A. 1/4
    B. 3/8
    C. 1/2
    D. 3/4

13. Structural capacities and design provisions for prefabricated wood I-joists shall be established and monitored in accordance with _____.

    A. ASTM E 2214
    B. APA 13A
    C. ASTM D 5055
    D. APWI 1525

14. The bracing required for each building shall be determined by circumscribing a rectangle around the entire building on each floor. The rectangle shall surround all enclosed offsets and projections such as sunrooms and attached garages. Open structures, such as carports and decks, shall be permitted to be excluded. The rectangle shall have no side greater than _____, and the ratio between the long side and short side shall be a maximum of _____.

    A. 160 feet (18 288 mm), 3:1
    B. 60 feet (18 288 mm), 3:1
  —C. 60 feet (18 288 mm), 4:1
    D. 120 feet (18 288 mm), 6:1

15. Openings which provide access to all under-floor spaces through a perimeter wall shall be not less than _____ inches .

  —A. 16 X 24
    B. 16 X 22
    C. 18 X 24
    D. 18 X 30

16. The greatest tread depth within any flight of stairs shall not exceed the smallest by more than _____ inch.

    A. .25
    B. 3/8
    C. .375
    D. B or C

17. Cleanout openings shall be provided within _____ inches of the base of each flue within every masonry chimney.

    A. 3
  →B. 6
    C. 12
    D. 24

18.   Handrail height, measured above the finished surface of the ramp slope, shall be not less than _____ inches and not more than _____ inches.

    A. 30, 42
    B. 34, 40
    C. 36, 42
    D. 34, 38

19.   Footings shall be _____ where it is necessary to change the elevation of the top surface of the footings or where the slope of the bottom surface of the footings will exceed one unit vertical in ten units horizontal.

    A. reinforced with rebar
    B. increased in depth
    C. leveled
    D. stepped

20.   Studs shall be continuous from support at the sole plate to a support at the top plate to resist loads perpendicular to the wall. The support shall be a foundation or floor, ceiling or roof diaphragm or shall be designed in accordance with _____.

    A. local traditional design
    B. maximum engineering values
    C. accepted engineering practice
    D. non of the above

21.   Emergency escape and rescue openings shall be operational from the inside of the room _____.

    A. keys, tools or special knowledge
    B. with three movements of the hand or less
    C. with outward force disengagement hardware
    D. all of the above

22.   Wood studs in nonbearing partitions may be notched to a depth not to exceed _____ percent of a single stud width.

A. 60
B. 35
C. 25
D. 40

23.   Lateral ties in masonry columns shall be spaced not more than _____ inches on center and shall be at least 3/8 inch diameter. Lateral ties shall be embedded in grout.

A. 4
B. 6
C. 8
D. 12

24.   Wood columns shall not be less in nominal size than _____ and steel columns shall not be less than 3-inch-diameter standard pipe or approved equivalent.

A. 4 inches by 4 inches
B. 3 inches by 3 inches
C. 6 inches by 6 inches
D. none of the above

25.   The building official, member of the board of appeals or employee charged with the enforcement of this code, while acting for the jurisdiction in good faith and without malice in the discharge of the duties required by this code or other pertinent law or ordinance, _____ for any damage accruing to persons or property as a result of any act or by reason of an act or omission in the discharge of official duties.

A. shall thereby be rendered liable personally and is hereby personally liability
B. shall not thereby be rendered liable personally and is hereby personally liability
C. shall thereby be rendered liable personally and is hereby relieved from personal liability
D. shall not thereby be rendered liable personally and is hereby relieved from personal liability

26.   Cold formed steel floor cantilevered joist shall be permitted only on the _____ of a two-story building or the first floor of a one-story building if the cantilevered joists are not doubled.

        A. first floor
        B. second floor

27.   There shall be a floor or landing at the _____ of each stairway. Exceptions ignored.

        A. top
        B. bottom
        C. top and bottom
        D. all of the above

28.   The requirements of this code are based on platform and _____ construction for light frame buildings.

        A. balloon frame
        B. wood frame
        C. steel frame
        D. all of the above

29.   For roof slopes of four units vertical in 12 units horizontal or greater, underlayment shall be a minimum of one layer of underlayment felt applied shingle fashion, parallel to and starting from the eaves and lapped _____ inches, fastened sufficiently in place.

        A. 1
        B. 2
        C. 4
        D. 6

30. The _____ shall include excavations for thickened slabs intended for the support of bearing walls, partitions, structural supports, or equipment and special requirements for wood foundations.

    A. floodplain inspections
    B. frame and masonry inspection
    C. foundation inspection
    D. none of the above

31. A nosing not less than _____ inch(es) but not more than _____ inch(es) shall be provided on stairways with solid risers.

    A. 1/2, 1-1/8
    B. 1, 1-1/2
    C. 5/8, 1-1/8
    D. 3/4, 1-1/4

32. The illumination of exterior stairways shall be controlled from _____ the dwelling unit.

    A. inside
    B. outside

33. Concrete and masonry foundation walls shall extend above the finished grade adjacent to the foundation at all points a minimum of _____ inches where masonry veneer is used and a minimum of _____ inches elsewhere.

    A. 6, 8
    B. 8, 10
    C. 4, 6
    D. 6, 4

34. Foam plastic, except where otherwise noted, shall be separated from the interior of a building by minimum _____ inch gypsum board or an approved finish material.

A. 3/8
B. 1/2
C. 5/8
D. 3/4

35.   What are the required steel reinforcement rods for an 8 inch thick masonry foundation wall with a height of 6 feet 8 inches with an unbalanced backfill height of 5 feet constructed in sandy gravel soil.

A. #3 at 48" o.c.
B. #4 at 48" o.c.
C. #4 at 60" o.c.
D. #4 at 72" o.c.

36.   Corrosion-resistant flashing at the base of an opening that is integrated into the building exterior wall to direct water to the exterior and is premanufactured, fabricated, formed or applied at the job site.

A. PAN FLASHING.
B. WINDOW WELL FLASHING
C. CORBLING FLASHING
D. DIVERSION FLASHING

37.   Rafters shall be framed to ridge board or to each other with a gusset plate as a tie The ridge board shall be at least ___ inch(es) nominal thickness and not less in depth than the cut end of the rafter.

A. 1
B. 2
C. 1.5
D. 4

38.   Utility grade studs shall not be spaced more than _____ inches on center, shall not support more than a roof and ceiling, and shall not exceed 8 feet in height for exterior walls and load-bearing walls or 10 feet for interior nonload-bearing walls.

A. 16
B. 19.2
C. 24
D. 32

39. Masonry chimneys shall be supported on foundations of solid masonry or concrete at least _____ inches thick and at least inches beyond each side of the exterior dimensions of the chimney.

   A. 12, 6
   B. 10, 5
   C. 16, 8
   D. 8, 6

40. Access shall be provided to all under-floor spaces with the minimum size of openings through the floor to be _____ inches .

   A. 16 X 22
   B. 18 X 30
   C. 18 X 24
   D. 22 X 30

41. Exterior landings, decks, balconies, stairs and similar facilities shall be positively anchored to the primary structure to resist both vertical and lateral forces or shall be designed to be self-supporting. Attachment shall not be accomplished by use of _____.

   A. joist hangers
   B. cantilevers
   C. lag bolts
   D. toenails

42. When the building official issues a permit, the construction documents shall be approved in writing or by a stamp which states _____.

   A. REJECTED
   B. APPROVED
   C. OK
   D. REVIEWED FOR CODE COMPLIANCE

43. A permit shall not be valid until the _____.

   A. fees have been paid
   B. plans are stamped
   C. construction has commenced
   D. day after issue

44. An application for a permit for any proposed work shall be deemed to have been abandoned _____ days after the date of filing, unless such application has been pursued in good faith or a permit has been issued.

   A. 45
   B. 90
   C. 180
   D. 360

45. Exhaust air shall not be directed onto _____.

   A. walkways
   B. the road
   C. beyond the minimum CFM
   D. a roof

46. A one story detached accessory structures with an area of less than _____ square feet does not require a permit.

   A. 100
   B. 200
   C. 300
   D. 400

47. Submittal documents consisting of construction documents, and other data shall be submitted in two or more sets with each application for a permit. The construction documents shall be prepared by a _____ where required by the statutes of the jurisdiction in which the project is to be constructed. Where special conditions exist, the building official is authorized to require additional construction documents to be prepared by a

_____.

A. licensed architect, licensed architect
B. licensed engineer, licensed engineer
C. registered design professional, registered design professional
D. any of these

48.   Fences less than _____ feet high do not require a permit.

    A. 4
    B. 7
    C. 8
    D. 10

49.   Tail joists over _____ feet long shall be supported at the header by framing anchors or on ledger strips not less than 2 inches by 2 inches.

    A. 8
    B. 10
    C. 12
    D. 14

50.   Each dwelling unit shall be provided with a kitchen area and every kitchen area shall be provided with a _____.

    A. refrigerator
    B. sink
    C. countertop
    D. all of the above

51.   The maximum riser height shall be _____ inches.

    A. 7.25
    B. 7.5
    C. 7.75
    D. 8

24

52.   What is the minimum thickness of lumber floor sheathing in inches, where the floor joists are spaced 16 inches OC and is installed perpendicular to the joist.

        A. 11/16
        B. 5/8
        C. 3/4
        D. 1/2

53.   Where a masonry or metal rain cap is installed on a masonry chimney, the net free area under the cap shall not be less than _____ the net free area of the outlet of the chimney flue it serves.

        A. two times
        B. three times
        C. four times
        D. ten times
        E. none of these

54.   Bathrooms shall have a minimum ceiling height of _____ at the center of the front clearance area for fixtures.

        A. 7 feet
        B. 6 feet 10 inches
        C. 6 feet 6 inches
        D. 7 feet 2 inches

55.   What is the weathering probability factor for the state of Wisconsin.

        A. Severe
        B. Moderate
        C. Negligible
        D. Extremely Severe

56.   In the case of demolition, the site plan shall show construction to be _____ and the location and size of existing structures and construction that are to remain on the site or plot. The building official is authorized to waive or modify the requirement for a site plan when the application for permit is for alteration or repair or when otherwise warranted.

A. erected
B. moved
C. demolished
D. none of these

57.   What is the minimum wall thickness in inches for a plain masonry foundation wall with a height of 9 feet with a unbalanced backfill height of 8 feet constructed in sand soil.

   A. 6
   B. 8
   C. 12
   D. 12 solid

58.   All egress doors shall be readily openable from the side from which egress is to be made without the use of a
_____.

   A. door knob
   B. panic hardware bar
   C. key or special knowledge or effort
   D. any of the above

59.   Ceilings in basements without habitable spaces may project to within _____ of the finished floor; and beams, girders, ducts or other obstructions may project to within _____ of the finished floor.

   A. 6 feet, 10 inches, 6 feet, 4 inches
   B. 6 feet, 10 inches, 6 feet, 8 inches
   C. 6 feet, 4 inches, 6 feet, 4 inches
   D. 6 feet, 8 inches, 6 feet, 4 inches

60.   A flight of stairs shall not have a vertical rise greater than _____ between floor levels or landings.

   A. 13 steps
   B. 12 feet
   C. 13 feet
   D. 12 steps

61.   Where equipment replacements and repairs must be performed in an emergency situation, _____.

        A. the permit application shall be submitted before any work can begin
        B. no permit is needed
        C. the permit application shall be submitted within the next working
business day
        D. none of the above

62.   The doubled cantilever back-span joists in cold-formed steel framed floors shall extend a minimum of _____ feet within the building.

        A. 2
        B. 4
        C. 6
        D. 8

63.   Habitable space, hallways, bathrooms, toilet rooms, laundry rooms and portions of basements containing these spaces shall have a ceiling height of not less than _____ feet

        A. 6.8
        B. 6
        C. 7
        D. 7.2

64.   What is the maximum ceiling joist span for SS Douglas fir-larch 2X8 spaced 19.2 inches OC with a live load of 20 PSF and a dead load of 10 PSF in an uninhabitable attics without storage.

        A. 17-1
        B. 18-5
        C. 24-0
        D. 15-2

65. Open sides of stairs with a total rise of more than 30 inches above the floor or grade below shall have guards not less than _____ inches in height measured vertically from the nosing of the treads.

    A. 32
    B. 34
    C. 36
    D. 42

66. Joists framing from opposite sides over a bearing support shall lap a minimum of _____ inches and shall be nailed together with a minimum _____ 10d face nails.

    A. 3, 1
    B. 4, 2
    C. 3, 3
    D. 4, 2

67. What is the fastener requirement for the wood ceiling joists to plate, toe nailed.

    A. 2-10d
    B. 3-10d
    C. 8-16d
    D. 3-8d

68. Enclosed accessible space under stairs shall have walls, under stair surface and any soffits protected on the enclosed side with 1/ 2 inch

_____.

    A. sheathing material
    B. gypsum board
    C. fiberboard or OSB
    D. any of the above

69. The wood sole plate at exterior walls on monolithic slabs and wood sill plate shall be anchored to the foundation with anchor bolts spaced a maximum of _____ feet on center.

A. 2
B. 4
C. 6
D. 8

70.   Steel fireplace units are permitted to be installed with solid masonry to form a masonry fireplace when installed either according to the requirements of their listing or according to the requirements of this section. Steel fireplace units incorporating a steel firebox lining, shall be constructed with steel not less than _____ inch in thickness, and an air circulating chamber which is ducted to the interior of the building.

A. 1/8
B. 1/4
C. 3/8
D. 1/16

71.   A roof covering composed of flat-plate photovoltaic modules fabricated into shingles.

A. GREEN ENERGY SHINGLES
B. ELECTRIC SOLAR BLANKET
C. LOW ENERGY MODULES
D. PHOTOVOLTAIC MODULES/SHINGLES

72.   All habitable rooms shall be provided with aggregate glazing area of not less than percent of the floor area of such rooms. Natural ventilation shall be through windows, doors, Exceptions ignored.

A. 4
B. 6
C. 8
D. 10

73.   Floor assemblies, not required elsewhere in this code to be fire-resistance rated, shall be provided with a _____ gypsum wallboard membrane, 5/8-inch (16 mm) wood structural panel membrane, or equivalent on the underside of the floor framing member. Exceptions ignored.

A. 3/8-inch (9.5 mm)
B. 1/2-inch (12.7 mm)
C. 5/8-inch (15.9 mm)
D. 3/4-inch (19.0 mm)

74.   A floor or landing is not required at the top of an interior flight of stairs, provided a door _____.

    A. has a safety catch type latch
    B. has a window allowing the occupant to see the stairway on the other side
    C. has a sign indicating that there is a stairway on the other side.
    D. does not swing over the stairs

75.   Stairways shall not be less than _____ inches in clear width at all points above the permitted handrail height and below the required headroom height.

    A. 30
    B. 32
    C. 36
    D. 44

76.   A composite of wood strand elements with wood fibers primarily oriented along the length of the member, where the least dimension of the wood strand elements is 0.10 inch (2.54 mm) or less and their average lengths are a minimum of 75 times and less than 150 times the least dimension of the wood strand elements.

    A. Laminated strand lumber (LSL)
    B. Parallel strand lumber (PSL)
    C. Oriented strand lumber (OSL)
    D. Laminated veneer lumber (LVL)

77.   What is the presumed load bearing value in pounds per square foot of silty sand,.

A. 2,000
B. 3,000
C. 4,000
D. 12,000

78.   Fireblocking of cornices of a two-family dwelling is required at
_____.

        A. between basement areas
        B. between garage areas
        C. 8 foot intervals
        D. at the line of dwelling unit separation

79.   The minimum width for concrete and masonry footings for a 2 story
conventional light frame construction dwelling where the soil load bearing value
is 3000 psf is _____ inches.

        A. 12
        B. 15
        C. 17
        D. 24

80.   Emergency escape and rescue openings with a finished sill height below
the adjacent ground elevation must be provided with a _____.

        A. handrail
        B. exit sign
        C. window well
        D. emergency lighting unit

81.   Reinforcement of web holes in cold steel formed floor joists not
conforming to the requirements of the IRC shall be permitted if the hole is
located fully within the center _____ percent of the span and the depth and
length of the hole does not exceed _____ percent of the flat width of the web.

        A. 25, 65
        B. 30, 50
        C. 40, 50
        D. 40, 65
        E. none of the above

82.   The maximum smoke-developed index of wall and ceiling finishes shall not exceed _____.

    A. 300
    B. 700
    C. 450
    D. 900

83.   The minimum thickness of masonry bearing walls more than one story high shall be _____ inches.

    A. 6
    B. 7
    C. 8
    D. 10

84.   What is the maximum span for a girder constructed of 4 2X8s douglas fir-larch a building 36 feet wide and supporting the roof, ceiling and one center-bearing floor. The ground snow load in the area is 30 psf.

    A. 4 feet 8 inches
    B. 5 feet 8 inches
    C. 5 feet 6 inches
    D. 6 feet 7 inches

85.   A minimum 3-foot-by-3-foot landing shall be provided for a ramp _____.

    A. At the top and bottom of ramps
    B. Where doors open onto ramps
    C. Where ramps change direction.
    D. All of the above
    E. None of the above

86.   Braced wall lines with a length of _____ or less shall have a minimum of two braced wall panels of any length or one braced wall panel equal to _____ or more. Braced wall lines greater than _____ shall have a minimum of two braced wall panels.

A. 16 feet (4877 mm) , 48 inches (1219 mm), 16 feet (4877 mm)
B. 16 feet (4877 mm) , 16 feet (4877 mm), 16 feet (4877 mm)
C. 16 feet (4877 mm) , 48 inches (1219 mm), 48 inches (1219 mm)
D. 48 inches (1219 mm) , 48 inches (1219 mm), 16 feet (4877 mm)

87.   Spiral stairways shall have all treads identical, and the rise shall be no more than _____ inches.

    A. 7 3/4
    B. 8 1/2
    C. 9
    D. 9 1/2

88.   What is the presumed load bearing value in pounds per square foot of crystalline bedrock.

    A. 1,500
    B. 2,000
    C. 4,000
    D. 12,000

89.   The fire-resistance-rated wall or assembly separating townhouses for townhouses shall be continuous from the foundation to the underside of the roof sheathing, deck or slab and shall extend the full length of the _____ including walls extending through and separating attached accessory structures.

    A. exterior walls
    B. wall or assembly
    C. joint wall
    D. non of the above

90.   How many jack studs are required under each end of a header made from 2 2X10s hem-fir supporting one floor only on a 28 foot wide building.   The ground snow load is 50 psf.

A. 1
B. 2
C. 3
D. 4

91.   In Townhouses, where roof surfaces adjacent to the wall or walls are at the same elevation, the parapet shall extend not less than _____ inches above the roof surfaces.

        A. 18
        B. 24
        C. 30
        D. 36

92.   Carports shall be open on _____.

        A. at least one side
        B. at least two sides
        C. at least three sides
        D. all four sides

93.   For roof slopes from two units vertical in 12 units horizontal up to _____ units vertical in 12 units horizontal, double underlayment application is required in accordance with Section R905.2.7.

        A. 3
        B. 4
        C. 5
        D. 6

94.   Egress doors shall be readily openable from inside the dwelling without the use of a _____ or special knowledge or effort.

        A. key
        B. bolt
        C. latch
        D. deadbolt

95. What is design temperature that should be used in calculating insulation values for central Illinois, in degrees Ferinheight.

    A. -10
    B. 0
    C. +10
    D. +20

96. Spiral stairways are permitted, provided the minimum width shall be _____ inches with each tread having a 71/2-inches minimum tread depth at 12 inches from the narrower edge.

    A. 26
    B. 30
    C. 32
    D. 36

97. The minimum width for concrete and masonry footings for a 1 story 8-inch solid or fully grouted masonry construction dwelling where the soil load bearing value is 1500 psf is _____ inches.

    A. 12
    B. 16
    C. 32
    D. 42

98. Every dwelling unit shall be provided with a water closet, lavatory, and a _____.

    A. bathtub
    B. shower
    C. bathtub or shower
    D. bathtub and shower

99. Footings on or adjacent to slope surfaces shall be founded in material with an embedment and setback from the slope surface sufficient to provide vertical and lateral support for the footing without detrimental settlement if the slope is steeper than one unit vertical in one unit horizontal, the required setback shall be measured from an imaginary plane _____ degrees to the horizontal, projected upward from the toe of the slope.

A. 15
B. 30
C. 45
D. 60

100. Portions of a room with a sloping ceiling measuring less than _____ feet or a furred ceiling measuring less than _____ feet from the finished floor to the finished ceiling shall not be considered as contributing to the minimum required habitable area for that room.

A. 4, 8
B. 5, 7
C. 4, 7
D. 3, 6

101. A single flat 2X4 member may be used as a header in interior or exterior nonbearing walls for openings up to _____ feet in width if the vertical distance to the parallel nailing surface above is not more than _____ inches.

A. 4, 12
B. 8, 24
C. 6, 18
D. 5, 24

102. Dwelling units in two-family dwellings shall be separated from each other by wall and/or floor assemblies having not less than _____ hour fire-resistance rating. Exceptions ignored.

A. 1/3
B. 1/2
C. 1
D. 2

103. Habitable rooms shall not be less than _____ feet in any horizontal dimension.

    A. 6
    B. 7
    C. 8
    D. 10

104. A stairway riser shall be measured vertically between leading edges of the adjacent treads with the greatest riser height within any flight of stairs not to exceed the smallest by more than _____ inch.

    A. .167
    B. .25
    C. .375
    D. .417

105. The smoke-developed rating shall _____ where foam plastic is used in a roof covering assembly without a thermal barrier when the foam is separated from the interior of the building by wood structural panel sheathing not less than 15/32 inch in thickness bonded with exterior glue and identified as Exposure 1, with edge supported by blocking or tongue-and-groove joints

    A. be not more than 450
    B. be not less than 450
    C. be not more than 600
    D. not be limited

106. Where enforcement of a code provision would violate the conditions of the listing of the equipment or appliance, appliance, the

_____.

    A. building official shall decide which provision shall apply.
    B. the board of review shall decide which provision shall apply.
    C. conditions of the listing and manufacturer's instructions shall apply
    D. None of the above

107.   No building or structure shall be used or occupied, and no change in the existing occupancy classification of a building or structure or portion thereof shall be made until the building official has issued a

_____ .

        A. notice of compliance
        B. use permit
        C. certificate of occupancy
        D. none of the above

108.   The total net free ventilating area of an attic shall not be less than 1 to _____ of the area of the space. Exceptions ignored.

        A. 50
        B. 100
        C. 150
        D. 200

109.   Where, in any specific case, different sections of this code specify different materials, methods of construction or other requirements, the _____ shall govern.

        A. least restrictive
        B. most restrictive
        C. most economical
        D. environmentally friendly

110.   Truss members and components shall not be cut, notched, spliced or otherwise altered in anyway without the approval of

_____.

        A. the IRC
        B. a professional contractor
        C. a residential designer
        D. a registered design professional.

111. Slabs on ground with turned down footings shall have a minimum of one _____ at the top and the bottom of the footing. Exceptions ignored.

    A. No. 3 bar
    B. No. 4 bar
    C. No. 5 bar
    D. No. 6 bar

112. _____ glazing in railings regardless of area or height above a walking surface are hazardous locations. Included are structural baluster panels and nonstructural infill panels.

    A. All
    B. 30 inch high
    C. 24 inch high
    D. 60 inch high

113. When the code refers to LIB bracing as a braced wall line method, what does LIB stand for?

    A. Lateral-inline-bracing
    B. Let-in-bracing
    C. Lumber-inline-bracing
    D. Lumber-internally-braced

114. A _____ inch thick base course consisting of clean graded sand, gravel, crushed stone or crushed blast-furnace slag passing a 2 inch sieve shall be placed on the prepared subgrade when the slab is below grade. Exceptions ignored.

    A. 2
    B. 3
    C. 4
    D. 5

115.   Joists exceeding a nominal _____ shall be supported laterally by solid blocking, diagonal bridging (wood or metal), or a continuous 1-inch-by-3-inch strip nailed across the bottom of joists perpendicular to joists at intervals not exceeding 8 feet. Exceptions ignored.

A. 2 x 12
B. 2 x 10
C. 2 x 8
D. 2 x 6

116.   All wood in contact with the ground, embedded in concrete in direct contact with the ground or embedded in concrete exposed to the weather that supports permanent structures intended for human occupancy shall be
_____. Exceptions ignored,

A. approved pressure preservative treated wood suitable for ground contact use
B. approved cedar or redwood
C. coated with 2 coats of black tar, creosote or formaldehyde.
D. any of the above

117.   An artificial light source is not required at the top and bottom landing, provided an artificial light source is located

_____.

A. adjacent to the stairway
B. at the beginning and end
C. directly over each stairway section
D. none of the above

118.   A handrail shall be provided on at least one side of all ramps exceeding a slope of one unit vertical in _____ units horizontal.

A. 6
B. 8
C. 10
D. 12

119. Any stud may be bored or drilled, provided that the diameter of the resulting hole is no greater than _____ percent of the stud width, the edge of the hole is no closer than 5/8 inch to the edge of the stud, and the hole is not located in the same section as a cut or notch. Exceptions ignored.

    A. 25
    B. 40
    C. 50
    D. 60

120. No person shall make connections from a utility, source of energy, fuel or power to any building or system that is regulated by this code for which a permit is required,

_____.

    A. until approved by the utility
    B. until approved by the building official
    C. until the permit is issued
    D. none of the above

121. The minimum width for concrete and masonry footings for a 2 story 4-inch brick veneer over light frame or 8-inch hollow concrete masonry construction dwelling where the soil load bearing value is 2000 psf is _____ inches.

    A. 12
    B. 16
    C. 21
    D. 24

122. Notches in solid lumber joists, rafters and beams shall not exceed _____ of the depth of the member, shall not be longer than one-third of the depth of the member and shall not be located in the middle one-third of the span.

    A. one-third
    B. one-fourth
    C. one-sixth
    D. one-fifth

123. Wood basement floors shall be limited to applications where the differential depth of fill on opposite exterior foundation walls is _____ feet or less, unless special provision is made to resist sliding caused by unbalanced lateral soil loads.

    A. 2
    B. 4
    C. 5
    D. 6

124. A three story dwelling is in a area that has a basic wind speed of 70 mph. The top floor of the structure uses the LIB method of bracing to resist the lateral wind forces. The Southern exterior braced wall line on this top floor has a braced wall line spacing of 30 feet. What is the minimum total length in feet of braced wall panels required along this braced wall line?

    A. 4.5
    B. 8.5
    C. 12
    D. 15.5

125. When there is usable space both above and below the concealed space of a floor/ceiling assembly, draftstops shall be installed so that the area of the concealed space does not exceed _____ square feet.

    A. 750
    B. 1,000
    C. 1,500
    D. 2,000

126. Which of the following is not listed as contained on a certificate of occupancy.

    A. The name of the contractor
    "B. Any special stipulations and conditions of the building permit."
    C. The name of the building official.
    D. The building permit number.

127. Before issuing a permit, the building official _____ or cause to be examined buildings, structures and sites for which an application has been filed.

    A. is authorized to examine
    B. must examine
    C. shall examine
    D. no authority to examine

128. The opening between adjacent treads is not limited on stairs with a total rise of _____ inches or less.

    A. 15
    B. 24
    C. 30
    D. 42

129. Dwelling units in two-family dwellings shall be separated from each other by wall and/or floor assemblies having not less than _____ hour fire-resistance rating if equipped throughout with an automatic sprinkler system installed in accordance with NFPA 13.

    A. 0
    B. 1/2
    C. 1
    D. 2

130. What is minimum specified compressive strength of concrete in psi for basement walls, foundation walls, exterior walls and other vertical concrete work exposed to the weather with moderate weathering potential.

    A. 1500
    B. 2000
    C. 3000
    D. 3500

131. All plumbing fixtures shall be connected to a sanitary sewer or to an
_____.

   A. approved private sewage disposal system
   B. holding tank
   C. gravity flow pipe system to the outdoors
   D. any of the above

132. What is the maximum rafter span for #1 Southern pine 2X8 spaced 16 inches OC with a ground snow load of 30 PSF and a dead load of 10 PSF with the ceiling not attached to the rafters.

   A. 14-7
   B. 14-7
   C. 18-1
   D. 19-9

133. Masonry chimney walls shall be constructed of solid masonry units or hollow masonry units grouted solid with not less than a _____ inch nominal thickness.

   A. 2
   B. 3
   C. 4
   D. 6

134. In geographical areas where experience has shows a specific need, approved naturally durable or pressure-preservative-treated wood may be used for those portions of the wood structure or other parts that form the structural supports of buildings, balconies, porches or similar permanent building part when those members are exposed to the elements without enough protection from a roof, eave, overhang or other covering that would inhibit moisture or water gathering on the surface or at joints between members. If Local experience dictates, these members can include:

   A. Horizontal members such as girders, joists and decking.
   B. Vertical members such as posts, poles and columns. 3.
   C. Both horizontal and vertical members.
   D. any or all of the above.

135.   Ducts in the garage and ducts penetrating the walls or ceilings separating the dwelling from the garage shall be constructed of a minimum No. _____ gage sheet steel or other approved material and shall have no openings into the garage.

    A. 30
    B. 24
    C. 26
    D. 20

136.   An alternative material, design or method of construction shall be approved where the building official finds that the proposed design is satisfactory and complies with the intent of the provisions of this code, and that the material, method or work offered is, for the purpose intended, _____.

    A. at least the equivalent of that prescribed in this code
    B. superior to that prescribed in this code
    C. even if it is not at least the equivalent of that prescribed in this code
    D. none of the above

137.   A comparative measure, expressed as a dimensionless number, derived from visual measurements of the spread of flame versus time for a material tested in accordance with ASTM E 84 or UL 723.

    A. FLAMABILITY INDEX
    B. FLAMABILITY TIME CONSTANT
    C. FLAME SPREAD INDEX
    D. NONE OF THESE

138.   Glazing in railings with and area of _____ sq. ft. or a height of _____ inches above a walking surface are considered hazardous locations.

    A. 9, 36
    B. 12, 42
    C. 6, 30
    D. All glazing in railings regardless of an area or height

139. What are the required steel reinforcement rods for an 12 inch thick masonry foundation wall with a height of 9 feet with a unbalanced backfill height of 8 feet constructed in SC soil.

    A. #6 at 48" o.c.
    B. #4 at 48" o.c.
    C. #5 at 48" o.c.
    D. #6 at 56" o.c.

140. Piping or ductwork placed in or partly in an exterior wall or interior load-bearing wall, necessitating cutting, drilling or notching of the top plate by more than 50 percent of its width, a galvanized metal tie of not less than _____ inches thick and 11/2 inches wide shall be fastened to each plate across and to each side of the opening with not less than _____ 10d nails having a minimum length of 11/2 inches (38 mm) at each side or equivalent.

    A. 0.054, 8
    B. 0.25, 8
    C. 0.054, 6
    D. 0.01, 4

141. All emergency escape and rescue openings shall have a minimum net clear opening width of _____ inches.

    A. 18
    B. 20
    C. 24
    D. 30

142. What is the maximum stud spacing of 2X6 bearing walls when supporting two floors, roof and ceiling (inches).

    A. 16
    B. 19.2
    C. 24
    D. 32

143.   When fire sprinklers are installed in a garage, is and overhead garage door considered to be an obstruction with respect to placement of the sprinkler heads?

    A. Yes
    B. No
    C. Overhead doors can not be used.
    D. Extra sprinkler heads must be used to cover the areas obstructed by the overhead door when open.

144.   For a truss framed roof in wind exposure category B, with the trusses spaces 16" OC, and a roof span of 28 feet, if the basic wind design speed is 100 mph what is the uplift force on the each truss connection to the top plate of the wall? The roof pitch is 12:12,

    A. 189
    B. 251
    C. 269
    D. 217

145.   Bathtub and shower floors and walls above bathtubs with installed shower heads and in shower compartments shall be finished with a nonabsorbent surface that extend to a height of not less than _____ above the floor.

    A. 6 feet
    B. 7 feet
    C. 6 feet 8 inches
    D. 6 feet 10 inches

146.   What is the maximum span for sanded plywood combination subfloor underlayment of Species Group 2 if the plywood is 3/4 inch thick.

    A. 16
    B. 20
    C. 24
    D. 32

47

147. A wood structural panel for a roof has a span rating of 32/16 it is 1/2 inch thick. What is the maximum span in inches for this panel if the edges are supported.

    A. 20
    B. 24
    C. 28
    D. 32

148. Openings in doors through which a _____ inch sphere is unable to pass is not considered a hazardous location with respect to glazing.

    A. 3
    B. 6
    C. 9
    D. 12

149. Footings shall not bear on frozen soil unless _____.

    A. they reinforced with a minimum of two #4 rebars placed 4" from the bottom of the footing.
    B. it is sandy gravel soil type
    C. footings are a minimum of 30 inches wide and 8 inches deep
    D. such frozen condition is of a permanent character

150. Doors between the garage and residence shall be equipped with solid wood doors not less than _____ inches in thickness, solid or honeycomb core steel doors not less than _____ inches thick, or _____ minute fire rated doors.

    A. 13/8, 13/8, 30
    B. 13/8, 13/8, 20
    C. 13/4, 13/4, 20
    D. 13/8, 13/8, 60

151. Handrails for stairways shall be continuous for the full length of the flight, from a point directly above the top riser of the flight to a point directly _____ lowest riser of the flight. Exceptions ignored.

A. above
B. perpendicular to the
C. parallel
D. none of the above

152. A comparative measure, expressed as a dimensionless number, derived from measurements of smoke obscuration versus time for a material tested in accordance with ASTM E 84 or UL 723.

A. FLAME TO SMOKE RATIO INDEX
B. SMOKE-DEVELOPED INDEX
C. TOXIC GAS INDEX
D. OBSURATION INDEX

153. The triangular openings formed by the riser, tread and bottom rail of a guard at the open side of a stairway are permitted to be of such a size that a sphere _____ inches cannot pass through.

A. 4
B. 6
C. 8
D. 12

154. Winder stairway treads shall have a minimum tread depth of _____ inches measured between the vertical planes of the foremost projection of adjacent treads at the intersections with the walkline.

A. 10
B. 9
C. 8
D. 9.5

155. Where lighting outlets are installed in interior stairways, there shall be a wall switch at each floor level to control the lighting outlet where the stairway has _____ or more risers.

    A. 3
    B. 4
    C. 5
    D. 6

156. Used materials, equipment and devices

_____.

    A. shall not be reused under any circumstance in new construction
    B. shall be reused if the general contractor will accept liability for material performance failure.
    C. shall not be reused unless approved by the building official
    D. none of the above

157. The ends of each joist, beam or girder shall have not less than _____ inches of bearing on metal. Exceptions ignored

    A. 1.5
    B. 2
    C. 3
    D. 4

158. What are the required steel reinforcement rods for an 10 inch thick foundation wall with a height of 9 feet with a unbalanced backfill height of 8 feet constructed in SC soil.

    A. #4 at 24" o.c.
    B. #4 at 48" o.c.
    C. #5 at 56" o.c.
    D. #6 at 40" o.c.

159.   Where it is necessary to make an inspection to enforce the provisions of this code, is authorized to enter the structure or premises at _____ to inspect or to perform the duties imposed by this code, provided that if such structure or premises be occupied that credentials be presented to the occupant and entry requested.

    A. any time
    B. unannounced
    C. reasonable times
    D. all of the above

160.   What is the minimum wall thickness in inches for a plain masonry foundation wall with a height of 8 feet with a unbalanced backfill height of 7 feet constructed in sandy gravel soil.

    A. 6
    B. 8
    C. 10
    D. 12

161.   Risers shall be vertical or sloped from the underside of the leading edge of the tread above at an angle not more than _____ degrees from the vertical.

    A. 15
    B. 30
    C. 45
    D. 60

162.   The minimum stairway tread depth shall be _____ inches.

    A. 9.25
    B. 10
    C. 10.5
    D. 11

163. The minimum openable area to the outdoors shall be _____ percent of the floor area being ventilated.

  A. 4
  B. 6
  C. 8
  D. 10

164. Handrails with a circular cross section shall have an outside diameter of at least _____ inches and not greater than _____ inches .

  A. 13/4, 2
  B. 11/4, 2 1/2
  C. 11/4, 2
  D. 1, 2 1/4

165. In dwellings or dwelling units with split levels and without an intervening door between the adjacent levels, a smoke alarm installed on the upper level shall suffice for the adjacent lower level provided that the lower level is less than _____.

  A. 4 feet below the upper level
  B. 8 feet below the upper level
  C. one full story below the upper level
  D. any of the above

166. Slate shingles shall only be used on slopes of _____ units vertical in 12 units horizontal or greater.

  A. 2
  B. 3
  C. 4
  D. 6

167. Garage floor surfaces shall be of approved _____ material.

  A. noncombustible
  B. concrete
  C. asphalt or concrete
  D. cement

168. What is minimum specified compressive strength of concrete in psi for porches, carport slabs and steps exposed to the weather, and garage floor slabs with severe weathering potential.

    A. 1500
    B. 2000
    C. 2500
    D. 3500

169. What is the maximum span for a header constructed of 3 2X8s douglas fir-larch a building 28 feet wide and supporting the two floors.

    A. 4 feet 5 inches
    B. 6 feet 7 inches
    C. 3 feet 6 inches
    D. 6 feet 3 inches

170. What is the maximum allowable span for #1 Spruce-pine-fir 2X6 floor joist space 19.2 inches OC with a live load of 40 psf and a dead load of 10 psf, in residential living areas.

    A. 9 feet 8 inches
    B. 8 feet 9 inches
    C. 10 feet 6 inches
    D. 7 feet 8 inches

171. Chimneys shall extend at least _____ feet higher than any portion of a building within _____ feet, but shall not be less than _____ feet above the highest point where the chimney passes through the roof.

    A. 3, 12, 6
    B. 4, 4, 3
    C. 2, 10, 3
    D. 2, 8, 3

172. Notches in flanges and lips of load-bearing steel floor framing members shall _____.

    A. be a maximum of 1/2 of the flange width
    B. be allowed if they are closer than 10 inches from bearing ends
    C. not be allowed
    D. none of these

173. What is the maximum allowable span for SS Douglas fir-larch 2X6 floor joist space 12 inches OC with a live load of 30 psf and a dead load of 10 psf, in residential sleeping areas.

    A. 10feet 8 inches
    B. 10feet 10 inches
    C. 12feet 6 inches
    D. 12feet 10 inches

174. When the header joist span exceeds _____ feet, the trimmer joists and the header joist shall be doubled and of sufficient cross section to support the floor joists framing into the header.

    A. 3
    B. 4
    C. 5
    D. 6

175. An exterior wall element is required to be fire-resistance rated, there is another structure less than 5 feet of the fire-resistance rated wall. Is this a violation of the code?

    A. Yes
    B. No
    C. Code does not apply here.
    D. not enough information to answer

176. The rough-framed opening for attic access shall not be less than _____ inches and shall be located in a hallway or other readily accessible location.

54

A. 18X22
B. 22X30
C. 24X30
D. 18X30

177. Handrails shall be permitted to be interrupted by a newel post
_____.

    A. at the turn
    B. only
    C. if the turn is more than 90 degrees
    D. none of the above

178. In dwelling units, where the opening of an operable window is located
more than 72 inches above the finished grade or surface below, the lowest part
of the clear opening of the window shall be a minimum of _____ inches
above the finished floor of the room in which the window is located.

    A. 4
    B. 6
    C. 8
    D. 12

R 312.2.1

P 63

24

179. The top flanges of steel joists shall be laterally braced by the application
of floor sheathing fastened to the joists. Floor joists with spans that exceed
_____ feet shall have the bottom flanges laterally braced.

    A. 6
    B. 8
    C. 12
    D. 14

180. Solid masonry walls of one-story dwellings and garages shall not be less
than _____ inches in thickness when not greater than _____ feet in height,
provided that when gable construction is used, an additional _____ feet is
permitted to the peak of the gable.

A. 9, 6, 6
B. 9, 6, 9
C. 8, 6, 6
D. 6, 9, 6

B. 8 6 9

181.   The concentration, rate of application and treatment method of the termiticide shall be in strict compliance with _____.

A. 5 lbs. per 100 sq ft
B. 10 lbs. per 100 sq ft
C. 20 lbs. per 100 sq ft
D. the termiticide label

182.   What is the maximum span for a girder constructed of 3 2X10s douglas fir-larch a building 28 feet wide and supporting the roof, ceiling and two clear span floors. The ground snow load in the area is 30 psf.

A. 5 feet 1 inches
B. 6 feet 4 inches
C. 5 feet 8 inches
D. 7 feet 6 inches

183.   Notches in solid lumber joists, rafters and beams shall not exceed _____ of the depth of the member, shall not be longer than _____ of the depth of the member and shall not be located in the middle _____ of the span.

A. one-sixth, one-third, one-half
B. one-third, one-third, one-third
C. one-sixth, one-third, one-third
D. one-sixth, one-half, one-third

184.   Where there is a conflict between a general requirement and a specific requirement, the _____ requirement shall be applicable.

A. specific
B. general
C. most general
D. least specific

56

185. The minimum width for concrete and masonry footings for a 2 story 4-inch brick veneer over light frame or 8-inch hollow concrete masonry construction dwelling where the soil load bearing value is 1500 psf is _____ inches.

    A. 12
    B. 16
    C. 21
    D. 24

186. Untreated wood may be used where

_____.

    A. painted properly
    B. partial submerged in fresh water
    C. entirely below groundwater level or continuously submerged in fresh water
    D. none of the above

187. Does a 200 square foot garage floor have to have a vapor retarder under the concrete slab?

    A. Yes
    B. No
    C. Only if it is not heated.
    D. Only if it is heated.

188. A (An) _____ residential fire sprinkler system shall be installed in one- and two- family dwellings.

    A. Copper or brass
    B. automatic
    C. remote control
    D. none of these

189. Winder stair treads shall have a minimum tread depth of _____ inches at any point.

   A. 6
   B. 8
   C. 10
   D. 12

190. Hollow concrete piers shall be capped with _____ of solid masonry or concrete, a masonry cap block, or shall have cavities of the top course filled with concrete or grout.

   A. 4 inches (102 mm)
   B. 6 inches (152 mm)
   C. 8 inches (203 mm)
   D. 12 inches (102 mm)

191. Garages beneath habitable rooms shall be separated from all habitable rooms above by not less than _____ or equivalent.

   A. 1/2 inch gypsum board
   B. 5/8 inch gypsum board
   C. 1/2 inch Type X gypsum board
   D. 5/8 inch Type X gypsum board

192. What is the maximum allowable span for a 4 × 3 × 1/4 lintel supporting masonry veneer with one story above.

   A. 8'-0"
   B. 6'-0"
   C. 4'-6"
   D. 3'-0"

193. Glazing in an individual fixed or operable panel adjacent to a door where the nearest vertical edge of the glazing is within a _____ inch arc of either vertical edge of the door in a closed position and where the bottom exposed edge of the glazing is less than _____ inches above the floor or walking surface shall be considered a hazardous location.

A. 24, 60
B. 78, 78
C. 72, 72
D. 48, 48

194. Within crawlspaces where entry is made only for service of utilities, foam plastics shall be protected against ignition by

_____,

A. 11/2-inch thick mineral fiber insulation or 1/4-inch hardboard
B. 1/4-inch thick wood structural panels or 3/8-inch gypsum board
C. 3/8-inch particle board, or corrosion-resistant steel having a base metal thick-ness of 0.016 inch
D. any or all of the above

195. What is the maximum allowable span for #3 Hem-fir 2X10 floor joist space 16 inches OC with a live load of 30 psf and a dead load of 20 psf, in residential sleeping areas.

A. 10feet 8 inches
B. 10feet 2 inches
C. 12feet 6 inches
D. 11feet 8 inches

196. The maximum total deflection of structural members that support glass unit masonry shall not exceed _____.

A. l/300
B. l/500
C. l/600
D. l/160

197.   When more than one smoke alarm is required to be installed within an individual dwelling unit the alarm devices shall be _____.

   A. independent
   B. within audible distance of each other
   C. placed a uniform distances within the dwelling
   D. interconnected

198.   In buildings with combustible ceiling or roof construction, an attic access opening shall be provided to attic areas that exceed _____ square feet and have a vertical height of _____ inches or greater.

   A. 30, 30
   B. 22, 30
   C. 18, 22
   D. 30, 22

199.   Where joists, trusses or rafters are spaced more than 16 inches on center and the bearing studs below are spaced 24 inches on center, such members shall bear within _____ inches of the studs beneath.

   A. 8
   B. 6
   C. 5
   D. 2

200.   With regard to wood floor framing, blocking shall be a minimum of utility grade lumber. Subflooring may be a minimum of utility grade lumber or _____ common grade boards.

   A. No. 1
   B. No. 2
   C. No. 3
   D. No. 4

201.   When the code refers to LIB bracing as a braced wall line method, what does LIB stand for?

A. Wind shear panel
B. Wood shear plywood
C. Wind structural-resistive panel
D. Wood structural panel

202.   Every landing where a stairway has a straight run shall have a minimum dimension of _____ measured in the direction of travel.

A. 36 inches
B. 32 inches
C. 44 inches
D. non of the above

203.   Where a stairway of _____ risers is located on the exterior side of a door, other than the required exit door, a landing is not required for the exterior side of the door.

A. two
B. two or fewer
C. three
D. two or fewer

204.   Handrail ends shall be returned or shall terminate in newel posts or

_____.

A. safety terminals
B. above the risers
C. at any point above the stairs
D. none of the above

205.   The provisions of the International Residential Code applies to the construction of detached one and two family dwellings and multiple single-family dwellings not more than _____ stories in height with a separate means of egress and their accessory structures.

A. one
B. two
C. three
D. four

206. What is minimum specified compressive strength of concrete basement walls in psi, foundations and other concrete not exposed to the weather with moderate weathering potential.

    A. 2500
    B. 3000
    C. 3500
    D. 3750

207. Every dwelling unit shall have at least one habitable room that shall have not less than _____ square feet of gross floor area.

    A. 90
    B. 100
    C. 120
    D. 180

208. When supported by steel-framed walls, cold-formed steel floor framing shall be constructed with floor joists located directly in-line with load-bearing studs located below the joists with a maximum tolerance of _____ inch between the center lines of the joist and the stud.

    A. 1/2
    B. 3/4
    C. 1
    D. 3/8

209. For the purpose of determining light and ventilation requirements, any room shall be considered as a portion of an adjoining room when at least 1/2 of the area of the common wall is open and unobstructed and provides an opening of not less than 1/10 of the floor area of the interior room but not less than _____ square feet.

    A. 25
    B. 50
    C. 75
    D. 100

210. The ends of each joist, beam or girder shall have not less than _____ inches of bearing on wood or metal. Exceptions ignored

    A. 3/4
    B. 1.5
    C. 3
    D. 4.5

211. What is the maximum stud spacing for nominal panel thickness of 7/16 inch wood structural panel wall sheathing used to resist wind pressures.

    A. 16
    B. 19.2
    C. 24
    D. 32

212. What is the minimum R value for insulation installed in a exterior building wood frame wall in a single family dwelling in Marathon County Wisconsin.

    A. R-21
    B. R-13
    C. R-19
    D. R20 or R13 + 5   p480
    E. C or D

213. In Table R502.3.1(1) Floor Joist Spans For Common Lumber Species (Residential Sleeping Areas, Live Load = 30 Psf, what maximum deflection are the values in the table based on.

    A. L/Δ = 360
    B. L/Δ = 240
    C. L/Δ = 120
    D. L/Δ = 180

214. For interior stairs the artificial light sources shall be capable of illuminating treads and landings to levels not less than _____ foot-candles measured at the center of treads and landings. Exceptions ignored.

A. 1
B. 2
C. 6
D. 10

215. The landing at an exterior doorway shall not be more than
_____ inches below the top of the threshold, provided the door, other
than an exterior storm or screen door does not swing over the landing.

A. .25
B. .75
C. 1.5
D. 7.75

216. Draftstopping shall divide the concealed space into
_____.

A. manageable flame spread areas
B. separate fire resistant domains
C. ventilation segments
D. approximately equal areas

217. Bathtub and shower floors and walls above bath tubs with installed
shower heads and in shower compartments shall be finished with
_____
.

A. ceramic tile
B. glass, tile, marble or other hard material
C. a nonabsorbent surface
D. a watertight enclosure

218. Wood-framed buildings shall be limited to _____ stories above grade
plane or the limits given in Table R602.10.3(3).

A. Two
B. Three
C. Four
D. Five

219. All exterior footings shall be placed at least _____ inches below the undisturbed ground surface.

    A. 12
    B. 16
    C. 20
    D. 24

220. All vertical joints of panel sheathing shall occur over, and be fastened to, common studs. Horizontal joints in braced wall panels shall occur over, and be fastened to, common blocking of a minimum _____ thickness.

    A. 11/2 inch (38 mm)
    B. 2 inch (50.8 mm)
    C. 1 inch (25.4 mm)
    D. 3/4 inch (19.0 mm)

221. Handrails adjacent to a wall shall have a space of not less than _____ inch between the wall and the handrails.

    A. 1- /2
    B. 1-1/4
    C. 2
    D. 1

222. What is the presumed load bearing value in pounds per square foot of silty clay.

    A. 1,500
    B. 2,500
    C. 3,500
    D. 4,000

223. It shall be the duty of the _____ to notify the building official that such work is ready for inspection.

A. permit holder or their agent
B. owner
C. contractor
D. none of the above

224.   At least one egress door shall be provided for each dwelling unit. The egress door shall be side-hinged, and shall provide a minimum clear width of _____ when measured between the face of the door and the stop, with the door open 90 degrees (1.57 rad).

A. 30 inches (762 mm)
B. 32 inches (813 mm)
C. 34 inches (864 mm)
D. 36 inches (914 mm)

225.   The radius of curvature at the leading edge of a tread shall be no greater than _____ inch.

A. 9/16
B. 1/2
C. 3/4
D. 1 1/4

226.   An automatic residential fire sprinkler system shall not be required when additions or alterations are made to _____ townhouses that do not have an automatic residential fire sprinkler system installed.

A. new single story
B. new slab on grade
C. existing
D. none of these

227.   On exterior walls that require bracing, walls parallel to a braced wall that are part of that bracing structure line shall be offset not more than _____ from the designated braced wall line location.

A. 1 foot (304 mm)
B. 2 feet (609 mm)
C. 4 feet (1219 mm)
D. 6 feet (1829 mm)

228.   A smoke alarm shall be installed outside each separate sleeping area in the immediate vicinity of _____.

    A. the garage
    B. the habitable rooms
    C. all areas of the dwelling
    D. the bedrooms

229.   Truss design drawings, shall be provided to the building official and approved _____.

    A. prior to installation
    B. at the job site
    C. after installation is completed
    D. none of the above

230.   _____ as required by this code, shall be available on the job site at the time of inspection.

    A. General Contractors license
    B. A list of contractors & sub-contractors
    C. Inspection certificates
    D. Manufacturer's installation instructions

231.   Smoke alarms shall receive their primary power from _____. Exceptions ignored.

    A. a emergency power source
    B. a battery UPS system
    C. the building wiring
    D. the battery within each unit

232. Beveling of stair nosing shall not exceed _____ inch.

A. 3/8
B. 1/2
C. 3/4
D. 1/4

233. Air exhaust and intake openings that terminate outdoors shall be protected with corrosion resistant screens, louvers or grilles having a minimum opening size of _____ inch and a maximum opening size of _____ inch in any dimension.

A. 1/8, 1/4
B. 1/2, 1
C. 1/4, 1/2
D. 3/8, 3/4

234. The diameter of holes bored or cut into members shall not exceed _____ the depth of the member.

A. 1/4
B. 1/3
C. 1/2
D. 2/3

235. All foam plastic or foam plastic cores used as a component in manufactured assemblies used in building construction shall have a flame-spread rating of not more than _____ and shall have a smoke-developed rating of not more than _____. Exceptions ignored.

A. 75, 450
B. 450, 75
C. 100, 350
D. 350, 100

236. A wood structural panel for a roof has a span rating of 24/16 it is 7/16 inch thick. What is the maximum span in inches for this panel if the edges are not supported.

A. 12
B. 16
C. 24
D. 28

237. The minimum horizontal area of the window well used as a emergency escape and rescue shall be _____ square feet, with a minimum horizontal projection and width of 36 inches.

A. 6
B. 9
C. 12
D. 15

238. Asphalt shingles shall only be used on roof slopes of _____ units vertical in 12 units horizontal or greater.

A. 2
B. 3
C. 4
D. 5

239. The ends of each rafter or ceiling joist shall have not less than _____ inches of bearing on wood or metal and not less than _____ inches on masonry or concrete.

A. 11/2, 3
B. 2, 4
C. 2, 3
D. 11/2, 4

240. The floor or landing at the exit door required by code shall not be more than _____ inches lower than the top of the threshold. Exceptions ignored.

A. .25
B. .75
C. 1.5
D. 7.75

241. For solid masonry units, solid grouted hollow units, or hollow units in anchored masonry veneer, wall ties shall be embedded in mortar bed at least

_____.

    A. 1 inch (25.4 mm)
    B. 2 inches (38 mm)
    C. 11/2 inches (50.8 mm)
    D. 3 inches (76.2mm)

242. What is the presumed load bearing value in pounds per square foot of sedimentary and foliated rock.

    A. 1,500
    B. 2,000
    C. 4,000
    D. 12,000

243. The walking surface of treads and landings of stairways shall be sloped no steeper than _____.

    A. 1-percent slope
    B. 2-percent slope
    C. 3-percent slope
    D. 4-percent slope

244. The ends of each joist, beam or girder shall have not less than _____ inches of bearing on masonry or concrete. Exceptions ignored

    A. 1.5
    B. 2
    C. 3
    D. 4

245.   Owner-occupied lodging houses with _____ guestrooms shall be permitted to be constructed in accordance with the International Residential Code for One- and Two-family Dwellings when equipped with a fire sprinkler system.

       A. two or fewer
       B. three or fewer
       C. four or fewer
       D. five or fewer

246.   Fire resistance rated floor ceiling and wall assemblies shall extend to and be tight against the exterior wall, and wall assemblies shall extend _____. Exceptions ignored.

       A. through the roof
       B. to the underside of the roof sheathing
       C. beyond the roof to a minimum height of 30 inches
       D. none of the above

247.   Which type of glazing my not be used in a skylight.

       A. Fully tempered glass.
       B. Heat strengthened glass.
       C. Double strength glass.
       D. Wired glass.

248.   What is the fastener requirement for the roof rafters to ridge, valley or hip rafters face nailed when using 16d nails.

       A. 2-16d
       B. 3-8d
       C. 3-16d
       D. 4-10d

249.   What is the maximum allowable span for cold-formed steel joists size 800S162-43 loaded with a live load of 40 PSF and spaced 16 inches OC.

A. 15'-6" 15'-4
B. 15'-6"
C. 12'-3"
D. 14'-1"

250. The minimum headroom above a spiral staircase is _____.

A. 6 feet 6 inches
B. 6 feet 8 inches
C. 6 feet 4 inches
D. 7 feet

251. The minimum width of a hallway shall be not less than

_____.

A. 3 feet
B. 38 inches
C. 36 inches
D. A and C

252. The minimum flange width in inches of cold formed steel joist with a web depth of 10 inches is _____.

A. 2
B. 1.75
C. 1.5
D. 1.625

253. What is the minimum thickness of lumber floor sheathing in inches, where the floor joists are spaced 24 inches OC and is installed perpendicular to the joist.

A. 11/16
B. 5/8
C. 3/4
D. 1

254.   Handrails shall not project more than _____ inches on either side of the stairway.

    A. 2.5
    B. 3
    C. 4
    D. 4.5

255.   For new construction, an approved _____ alarm shall be installed outside of each separate sleeping area in the immediate vicinity of the bedrooms in dwelling units within which fuel-fired appliances are installed and in dwelling units that have attached garages.

    A. carbon dioxide
    B. carbon monoxide
    C. greenhouse gas
    D. methane gas

256.   Slump of concrete placed in removable forms shall not exceed _____. Exceptions ignored.

    A. 4 inches (101mm)
    B. 6 inches (152 mm)
    C. 8 inches (203 mm)
    D. 12 inches (304 mm)

257.   All unit skylights installed in a roof with a pitch flatter than _____ units vertical in 12 units horizontal shall be mounted on a curb extending at least _____ inches above the plane of the roof unless otherwise specified in the manufacturer's installation instructions.

    A. two, 6
    B. three, 6
    C. four, 6
    D. three, 4

258.   When the header joist span does not exceed _____ feet, the header joist may be a single member the same size as the floor joist.

A. 3
B. 4
C. 5
D. 6

259. Marathon County Wisconsin is in which energy conservation climate zone.

A. 3A
B. 4B
C. 6A
D. 7

260. Type GW soil is a Group _____ soil group member.

A. I
B. II
C. III
D. IV

261. Handrails with a perimeter greater than _____ inches shall provide a graspable finger recess area on both sides of the profile.

A. 4
B. 5.5
C. 6
D. 61/4

262. What is the maximum ceiling joist span for #2 Hem-fir 2X8 spaced 12 inches OC, with a live load of 10 PSF and a dead load of 5 PSF in an uninhabitable attics without storage.

A. 10-3
B. 15-10
C. 18-2
D. 24-0

263.   Buildings shall have approved address numbers, building numbers or approved building identification placed in a position that is plainly legible and visible from the street or road fronting the property. These numbers shall contrast with their background. Address numbers shall be Arabic numbers or alphabetical letters. Numbers shall be a minimum of _____ high with a minimum stroke width of _____. Where access is by means of a private road and the building address cannot be viewed from the public way, a monument, pole or other sign or means shall be used to identify the structure.

   A. 3 inches (77 mm), 1/2 inch (12.7 mm)
   B. 4 inches (102 mm), 1/2 inch (12.7 mm)
   C. 4 inches (102 mm), 1/4 inch (6.4 mm)
   D. 6 inches (153 mm), 1/2 inch (12.7 mm)

264.   The grade away from foundation walls shall fall a minimum of_____ inches within the first _____ feet. Exceptions ignored.

   A. 10, 6
   B. 8, 12
   C. 12, 12
   D. 6, 10

265.   The building official shall issue all necessary _____ to ensure compliance with this code.

   A. permits
   B. certificates
   C. restrictions
   D. notices or orders

266.   The building official shall receive applications, review construction documents and issue permits for the erection and alteration of buildings and structures, inspect the premises for which such permits have been issued and _____.

   A. reject any provision of this code he sees fit
   B. enforce compliance with the provisions of this code
   C. add any articles he feels the code is lacking
   D. all of the above

267. The use of a volute, turnout, starting easing or starting newel shall be allowed over the _____ tread.

    A. last
    B. first
    C. first and last
    D. lowest

268. Carports not open on _____ side(s) shall be considered a garage and shall comply with the provisions of this section for garages.

    A. one
    B. two
    C. three
    D. all four

269. Flue lining systems for gas appliances shall be in accordance with Chapter _____.

    A. 20
    B. 23
    C. 24
    D. 27

270. What is the maximum cantilever span for 2X10 floor joists 24 inches oc, with a ground snow load of 50 psf.

    A. 20 inches
    B. 40 inches
    C. 48 inches
    D. 60 inches

271. Foam-filled doors _____ from the requirements of Section R314.1.

    A. are exempt
    B. are included

272. What is the maximum allowable span for cold-formed steel joists size 1200S162-54 loaded with a live load of 30 PSF and spaced 16 inches OC.

    A. 23'- 4"
    B. 19'-7"
    C. 21'-3"
    D. 17'-6"

273. Basements and every sleeping room shall have at least

_____ .

    A. one openable emergency escape and rescue opening
    B. two openable emergency escape and rescue openings
    C. one emergency escape and rescue opening
    D. two openable emergency escape and rescue opening

274. What is the minimum wall thickness in inches for a plain masonry foundation wall with a height of 7 feet with a unbalanced backfill height of 4 feet constructed in sandy clay soil.

    A. 5
    B. 6
    C. 7
    D. 8

275. A wood structural panel for a subfloor has a span rating of 24/16 it is 7/16 inch thick. What is the allowable live load in psf for this panel if the floor joists are spaced 16" o.c.

A. 30
B. 50
C. 100
D. 180

276.   All emergency escape and rescue openings shall have a minimum net clear opening of _____ square feet. Exceptions ignored.

A. 3.2
B. 9
C. 5.7
D. 7.5

277.   Wood foundation basements shall be drained and _____ in accordance with Sections R405 and R406, respectively.

A. dampproofed
B. waterproofed
C. rainproofed
D. none of the above

278.   The minimum width for concrete and masonry footings for a 3 story 8-inch solid or fully grouted masonry construction dwelling where the soil load bearing value is 1500 psf is _____ inches.

A. 12
B. 21
C. 29
D. 42

279.   Joists framing into the side of a wood girder shall be supported by approved framing anchors or on ledger strips not less than nominal _____.

A. 2 X 2
B. 2 X 4
C. 1 X 4
D. 2 X 6

280. Any wood stud in an exterior wall or bearing partition may be cut or notched to a depth not exceeding _____ percent of its width.

A. 25
B. 35
C. 40
D. 60

281. _____ is required at all interconnections between concealed vertical and horizontal spaces such as occur at soffits, drop ceilings and cove ceilings.

A. Draftstopping
B. Smoke barriers
C. Fireblocking
D. non of the above

282. Where eave or cornice vents are installed, insulation shall not block the free flow of air so that a minimum of a _____ inch(es) space shall be provided between the insulation and the roof sheathing at the location of the vent.

A. 1
B. 2
C. 3
D. 4

283. Open stair risers are permitted if the opening between treads does not permit the passage of a _____ inch diameter sphere.

A. 4
B. 6
C. 7
D. 8

284. There shall be a floor or landing _____ of each exterior door. Exceptions ignored.

A. on the inside
B. on the outside
C. on either the inside or outside
D. on each side

285.   Beams, girders or other concentrated loads supported by a wall or column shall have a bearing of at least 3 inches in length measured parallel to the beam upon solid masonry not less than _____ inches in thickness, or upon a metal bearing plate of adequate design and dimensions to distribute the load safely, or upon a continuous reinforced masonry member projecting not less than 4 inches from the face of the wall.

      A. 1.5
      B. 2
      C. 3
      D. 4

286.   Insulation materials, including facings, such as vapor retarders or vapor permeable membranes installed within floor-ceiling assemblies, roof-ceiling assemblies, wall assemblies, crawl spaces and attics shall have a flame-spread index not to exceed _____ with an accompanying smoke-developed index not to exceed. Exceptions ignored.

      A. 25, 450
      B. 50, 600
      C. 65, 450
      D. 25, 200

287.   Bars, grills, covers, screens or similar devices are permitted to be placed over emergency escape and rescue openings, bulkhead enclosures, or windowwells that serve such openings, provided the minimum net clear opening size complies with the code and such devices shall be _____ from the inside without the use of a key, tool, special knowledge or force greater than that which is required for normal operation of the escape and rescue opening.

      A. releasable
      B. removable
      C. releasable or removable
      D. any of the above

288.   If any concealed trap, drain pipe, water, soil, waste or vent pipe becomes defective and it becomes necessary to remove and replace the same with new material, such work shall be considered as

_____.

A. old work no permit is needed
B. new work and a permit shall be obtained
C. existing work
D. none of the above

289.   "The IRC Code regulates the construction of steel floor framing for buildings not greater than _____ feet in length perpendicular to the joist span, not greater than _____ feet in width parallel to the joist span, and less than or equal to _____ stories above grade plane"

A. 60, 60, 2
B. 60, 28,3
C. 60, 40, 3
D. 40, 36, 3

290.   Single trimmer joists may be used to carry a single header joist that is located within _____ feet of the trimmer joist bearing.

A. 3
B. 4
C. 5
D. 6

291.   Handrails shall be provided on at least one side of each continuous run of treads or flight with _____ or more risers.

A. two
B. three
C. four
D. six

292.   What is the fastener requirement for the blocking between wood joists or rafters to top plate, toe nail.

A. 3-8d
B. 4-8d
C. 3-10d
D. 4-10d

293.   The garage shall be separated from the residence and its attic area by not less than _____ applied to the garage side.

   A. 5/8-inch Type X gypsum board or equivalent
   B. 1/2-inch gypsum board or equivalent
   C. 3/4 inch fiberboard, plywood or 1/2 gypsum board
   D. non of the above

294.   The required quality mark on each piece of pressure preservatively treated lumber or plywood shall contain which of the following information.

      A. Identification of the treating plant, type of preservative, the minimum preservative retention end use for which the product was treated
      B. Standard to which the product was treated, identity of the approved inspection agency
      C. identity of the approved inspection agency, the designation "Dry", if applicable.
      D. all of the above

295.   The construction of buildings and structures in accordance with the provisions of this code shall result in a system that provides a complete load path that meets all requirements for the transfer of all loads from their point of origin through the load resisting elements to the _____.

   A. floor
   B. exterior walls
   C. building structure
   D. foundation

296.   Openings from a private garage directly into a room used for sleeping purposes _____.

A. must be protected by a minimum 20 minute fire rated covering.

B. must have a 1- 3/8 inch self closing door with a 20 minute fire rating.

C. are limited to single leaf swinging doors with 20 minute fire rating.

D. shall not be permitted

297. Foam plastics may be used without a thermal barrier when the foam plastic is protected by a minimum _____ inch(es) thickness of masonry or concrete.

A. 1

B. 2

C. 3

D. 4

298. Wood columns shall be approved

_____. Exceptions ignored.

A. wood of natural decay resistance

B. pressure preservatively treated wood

C. either of the above

D. none of the above

299. For a truss framed roof in wind exposure category B, with the trusses spaces 24" OC, and a roof span of 32 feet, if the basic wind design speed is 90 mph what is the uplift force on the each truss connection to the top plate of the wall? The roof pitch is 5:12,

A. 50

B. 200

C. 150

D. 175

300. What is the minimum wall thickness in inches for a plain masonry foundation wall with a height of 6 feet with a unbalanced backfill height of 5 feet constructed in sandy gravel soil.

A. 6 solid or 8

B. 10 solid

C. 12

D. 10

301. On a wall that required braced wall line, if there is a diagonal wall section and the section is longer than _____ feet, then it must be treated as a separate braced wall line.

    A. 4
    B. 6
    C. 8
    D. 12

302. Where work requiring a permit occurs in existing dwellings that have attached garages or in existing dwellings within which _____ exist, carbon monoxide alarms shall be provided.

    A. baseboard resistance heating appliances
    B. refrigerator freezers
    C. fuel-fired appliances
    D. all of these

303. All emergency escape and rescue openings shall have a minimum net clear opening height of _____ inches.

    A. 18
    B. 24
    C. 30
    D. 36

304. The bottom surface of footings shall not have a slope exceeding one unit vertical in _____ units horizontal .

    A. 12
    B. 10
    C. 6
    D. 8

305. Wood shingles shall be installed on slopes of three units vertical in _____ percent slope or greater.

A. 10
B. 20
C. 25
D. 40

306. Loose-fill insulation materials that cannot be mounted in the ASTM E 84 apparatus without a screen or artificial supports shall have a flame-spread rating not to exceed _____ with an accompanying smoke-developed factor not to exceed . Exceptions ignored.

A. 50, 500
B. 25, 450
C. 75, 400
D. none of the above

307. Wood framing supporting gypsum board shall not be less than _____ inches nominal thickness in the least dimension except that wood furring strips not less than 1X2 inch nominal dimension may be used over solid backing or framing spaced not more than _____ inches on center.

A. 2, 24
B. 4, 16
C. 3, 16
D. 1.5, 16

308. What are the required steel reinforcement rods for an 12 inch thick masonry foundation wall with a height of 8 feet with a unbalanced backfill height of 6 feet constructed in GM soil.

A. #5 at 56" o.c.
B. #4 at 72" o.c.
C. #6 at 72" o.c.
D. #4 at 56" o.c.

309. What are the required steel reinforcement rods for an 9.5 inch thick concrete foundation wall with a height of 8 feet with a unbalanced backfill height of 7 feet constructed in GM soil.

A. #4 at 24" o.c.
B. #4 at 32" o.c.
C. #6 at 32" o.c.
D. Plain Concrete, none

310. All exposed insulation materials installed on attic floors shall have a critical radiant flux not less than _____ watt per square centimeter.

A. 0.12
B. 0.25
C. 1.25
D. 3.75

311. Backfill shall not be placed against the wall until the wall has sufficient strength and has been anchored to the floor above, or has been sufficiently _____ to prevent damage by the backfill.

A. anchored
B. examined
C. braced
D. none of the above

312. Ends of ceiling joists shall be lapped a minimum of _____ inches or butted over bearing partitions or beams and toenailed to the bearing member.

A. 2
B. 3
C. 4
D. 6

313. What is the minimum thickness of lumber floor sheathing in inches, where the floor joists are spaced 54 inches OC and is installed perpendicular to the joist.

A. 11/16 T&G
B. 3/4 T&G
C. 5/8 T&G
D. 1-1/2 T&G

314. _____ shall be permitted to be backfilled prior to inspection.

    A. Underground plumbing pipes
    B. Under slab electrical conduits and raceways
    C. Under slab gas piping
    D. Ground-source heat pump loop systems tested in accordance with Section M2105.1

315. Glazing in walls, enclosures or fences containing or facing hot tubs, spas, whirlpools, saunas, steam rooms, bathtubs, showers and indoor or outdoor swimming pools where the bottom exposed edge of the glazing is less than _____ inches (1524 mm) measured vertically above any standing or walking surface shall be considered a hazardous location. This shall apply to single glazing and all panes in multiple glazing. Exceptions ignored.

    A. 96
    B. 72
    C. 60
    D. 48

316. Single station carbon monoxide alarms shall be listed as complying with _____ and shall be installed in accordance with this code and the manufacturer's installation instructions.

    A. UL 2034
    B. CE 4582
    C. NFPA Alarm code
    D. Any of these

317. Joists shall be supported laterally at the ends by full-depth solid blocking not less than _____ inches nominal in thickness; or by attachment to a full depth header, band, or rim joist, or to an adjoining stud, or shall be otherwise provided with lateral support to prevent rotation. Exceptions ignored.

    A. 1
    B. 2
    C. 3
    D. 4

318.   Freestanding accessory structures with an area of _____ square feet or less and an eave height of 10 feet or less shall not be required to be protected from frost.

    A. 100
    B. 200
    C. 300
    D. 400

319.   What is the maximum rafter span for #1 S-P-F 2X12 spaced 16 inches OC with a ground snow load of 30 PSF and a dead load of 20 PSF with the ceiling not attached to the rafters.

    A. 16-6
    B. 13-6
    C. 23-6
    D. 19-2

320.   The minimum net required ventilation for a crawl space under any building shall be provided with ventilation openings through foundation walls or exterior walls which are at least 1 square foot of area for each _____ square feet of under-floor space area, unless the ground surface is covered by a Class 1 vapor retarder material.

    A. 150
    B. 100
    C. 75
    D. 50

321.   What is the cross-sectional area of a round flue 8 inches in diameter (answer is in square inches)

    A. 28
    B. 38
    C. 50
    D. 64

322.   Work shall not be done beyond the point indicated in each successive inspection without first obtaining _____.

    A. a permit for that section
    B. contractors approval
    C. the approval of the building official
    D. none of the above

323.   The width of a landing can not be less than the door served and every landing shall have a minimum dimension of _____ inches measured in the direction of travel.

    A. 36
    B. 40
    C. 44
    D. 48

324.   All smoke alarms shall be installed in accordance with the provisions of this code and the household fire warning equipment provisions of

_____.

    A. NFPA 13
    B. IRC 72
    C. NFPA 72
    D. none of the above

325.   The building official is authorized to engage _____ as deemed necessary to report upon unusual technical issues that arise, subject to the approval of the appointing authority.

    A. an expert opinion
    B. in exploration
    C. scientific experiments
    D. none of the above

326. Each townhouse shall be _____ and shall be separated by fire resistance rated wall assemblies meeting the requirements of Section R302 for exterior walls. Exceptions ignored.

A. considered a separate building
B. considered part of the same building
C. fire resistance dependent on the other unit.
D. none of the above

327. What is the maximum allowable length (in feet) of wood wall studs exposed to wind speeds of 100 mph or less in seismic design categories a, b, c and d, for 2X6 studs supporting one floor and a roof 16 inches OC.

A. 10
B. 12
C. 16
D. 18

328. Which of the following does not require a permit.

A. Prefabricated swimming pools that are less than 36 inches deep.
B. Swings and other playground equipment.
C. Window awnings supported by an exterior wall which do not project more than 80 inches from the exterior wall and do not require additional support.
D. all of the above

329. All spaces between chimneys and floors and ceilings through which chimneys pass shall be _____ with noncombustible material securely fastened in place.

A. fireproofed
B. smokeproofed
C. fireblocked
D. any of the above

330. Subflooring may be omitted when joist spacing does not exceed _____ inches and a 1-inch nominal tongue-and-groove wood strip flooring is applied perpendicular to the joists.

    A. 12
    B. 16
    C. 19.2
    D. 24

331. Smoke alarms shall be installed in which of the following locations.

    A. In each sleeping room
    B. Outside each separate sleeping area in the immediate vicinity of the bedrooms
    C. On each additional story of the dwelling, including basements but not including crawl spaces and uninhabitable attics
    D. all of the above

332. A stud may be bored to a diameter not exceeding _____ percent of its width, provided that such studs located in exterior walls or bearing partitions are and are bored over _____ percent that they be doubled and that not more than two successive studs are bored.

    A. 25, 10
    B. 40, 35
    C. 60, 40
    D. 75, 60

333. The minimum thickness of galvanized steel valley lining material is _____ inches nominal.

    A. 0.0279
    B. 0.0379
    C. 0.0479
    D. 0.0179

334. Where basements contain one or more sleeping rooms, emergency egress and rescue openings shall be required in each sleeping room, _____.

    A. but shall not be required in adjoining areas of the basement
    B. and shall also be required in adjoining areas of the basement
    C. unless there are emergency egress and rescue openings in adjoining areas of the basement
    D. none of the above

335. Bathrooms, water closet compartments and other similar rooms shall be provided with aggregate glazing area in windows of not less than _____ square feet, one-half of which must be openable. Exceptions ignored.

    A. 3
    B. 6
    C. 9
    D. 12

336. Flanges and lips of load-bearing cold-formed steel roof framing members _____.

    A. may be notched but not cut
    B. may be cut but not notched
    C. may be cut or notched
    D. shall not be cut or notched

337. Every permit issued shall become invalid unless the work authorized by such permit is commenced within _____ days after its issuance, or if the work authorized by such permit is suspended or abandoned for a period of _____ days after the time the work is commenced.

    A. 45, 90
    B. 90, 180
    C. 180, 180
    D. 365, 180

338.   The purpose of the IRC is to establish _____
requirements to safeguard the public safety, health and general welfare through
affordability, structural strength, means of egress facilities, stability, sanitation,
light and ventilation, energy conservation and safety to life and property from
fire and other hazards attributed to the built environment and to provide safety
to fire fighters and emergency responders during emergency operations.

    A. standard
    B. maximum
    C. minimum
    D. limited

339.   Hearth extensions shall extend at least _____ inches front of and at
least _____ inches beyond each side of the fireplace opening, where the
fireplace opening is 6 square feet or less.

    A. 12, 12
    B. 20, 10
    C. 24, 6
    D. 16, 8

340.   Foam plastic may be used in a roof covering assembly without a thermal
barrier when the foam is separated from the interior of the building by wood
structural panel sheathing not less than _____ inch in thickness bonded with
exterior glue and identified as Exposure 1, with edge supported by blocking or
tongue-and-groove joints.

    A. 15/32
    B. 1
    C. 1-15/32
    D. 1-3/4

341.   An enclosed attic has a square footage of 2833 sf. What is the minimum
free ventilation area required to vent this space. Exceptions ignored

    A. 6.3 sf
    B. 9.6 sf
    C. 18.9 sf
    D. 27.3 sf

342.   Foundation cripple walls shall be framed of studs not less in size than the studding above and when exceeding _____ feet in height, such walls shall be framed of studs having the size required for an additional story.

    A. 3
    B. 4
    C. 5
    D. 6

343.   Which of the following locations is not always considered specific hazardous locations for the purposes of glazing.

    A. Glazing in storm doors
    B. Glazing in swinging doors except jalousies
    C. Glazing in fixed and sliding panels of sliding door assemblies and panels in sliding and bifold closet door assemblies
    D. Decorative glazing.
    E. All of the above

344.   Columns shall be restrained to prevent lateral displacement at the _____ end(s).

    A. bottom
    B. top
    C. both
    D. any of the above

345.   What is the maximum spacing for framing members for a ceiling with 5/8" gypsum board applied parallel to the framing members.

    A. 16
    B. 19.2
    C. 24
    D. 28

346.   Fasteners for pressure preservative and fire-retardant-treated wood shall be _____.

    A. steel or iron
    B. screws only
    C. hot-dipped galvanized steel, stainless steel, silicon bronze or copper.
    D. stainless steel only

347. Which of the following does not require a permit.

A. Retaining walls that are not over 4 feet in height measured from the bottom of the footing to the top of the wall, unless supporting a surcharge.
B. Water tanks supported directly upon grade if the capacity does not exceed 5,000 gallons and the ratio of height to diameter or width does not exceed 2 to 1.
C. Sidewalks and driveways.
D. Painting, papering, tiling, carpeting, cabinets, counter tops and similar finish work.
E. all of the above

348. Floor cantilevers in cold-formed steel framing shall not exceed _____ inches.

A. 12
B. 24
C. 36
D. 48

349. Basic wind speed is defined as a _____ second gust speed at 33 feet above the ground in wind exposure C .

A. one
B. three
C. ten
D. sixty

350. The building official is authorized to make all of the required inspections, or the building official shall have the authority to

_____.

A. receive signed affidavits by the owner or contractor
B. accept reports of inspection by approved agencies or individuals
C. wave any and all inspections
D. none of the above

351. When alterations, repairs or additions requiring a permit occur, or when one or more sleeping rooms are added or created in existing dwellings, the individual dwelling unit shall be equipped with smoke alarms located as required for new dwellings unless the permit is for work _____,

    A. involving the exterior surfaces of dwellings, such as the replacement of roofing or siding.
    B. the addition or replacement of windows or doors.
    C. the addition of a porch or deck as in the 2009 INTERNATIONAL RESIDENTIAL CODE® BUILDING PLANNING.
    D. any of the above

352. A common _____ hour fire resistance rated wall is permitted for townhouses if such walls do not contain plumbing or mechanical equipment, ducts or vents in the cavity of the common wall.

    A. 1/3
    B. 1/2
    C. 1
    D. 2

353. Handrail height, measured vertically from the sloped plane adjoining the tread nosing, or finish surface of ramp slope, shall be not less than _____ inches and not more than _____ inches. Exceptions ignored.

    A. 30, 40
    B. 32, 36
    C. 36, 40
    D. 34, 38

354. The minimum headroom over a stairway shall not be less than _____ measured vertically from the sloped plane adjoining the tread nosing or from the floor surface of the landing or platform.

    A. 6 feet 4 inches
    B. 6 feet 8 inches
    C. 6 feet 10 inches
    D. 7 feet

355. What is the presumed load bearing value in pounds per square foot of sandy gravel and/or gravel.

    A. 1,000
    B. 1,500
    C. 3,000
    D. 4,000

356. What is the maximum span for a header constructed of 2 2X6s southern pine in building 28 feet wide and supporting the roof and ceiling. The ground snow load is 50 psf.

    A. 3 feet 11 inches
    B. 4 feet 1 inches
    C. 3 feet 6 inches
    D. 4 feet 8 inches

357. Where lot lines, walls, slopes or other physical barriers prohibit _____ inches of fall within 10 feet for surface drainage, Impervious surfaces within 10 feet (3048 mm) of the building foundation shall be sloped a minimum of _____ percent away from the building

    A. 4, 5
    B. 6, 2
    C. 8, 2
    D. 10, 6

358. The building official is hereby authorized and directed to enforce the provisions of this code and he shall have the authority to _____ of this code and to adopt policies and procedures in order to clarify the application of its provisions.

    A. render interpretations
    B. modify the articles
    C. wave sections in the enforcement
    D. none of the above

359. The maximum slope for a ramp is one unit vertical in _____ units horizontal.

A. twelve
B. ten
C. eight
D. six

360. This describes type SP soil type.

A. Well-graded gravels, gravel sand mixtures, little or no fines.
B. Poorly graded gravels or gravel sand mixtures, little or no fines.
C. Well-graded sands, gravelly sands, little or no fines.
D. Poorly graded sands or gravelly sands, little or no fines.

361. Stairway tread depth shall be measured horizontally between the vertical planes of the foremost projection of adjacent treads and _____ to the tread's leading edge.

A. at a right angle
B. 90 degrees
C. perpendicular
D. all of the above

362. What is the maximum span for a header constructed of 3 2X12s douglas fir-larch a building 20 feet wide and supporting the roof, ceiling and two center-bearing floors. The ground snow load is 70 psf.

A. 4 feet 5 inches
B. 5 feet 4 inches
C. 6 feet 6 inches
D. 7 feet 8 inches

363. When ceiling joists are used to provide resistance to rafter _____, lapped joists shall be nailed together in accordance with this section and butted joists shall be tied together in a manner to resist such _____.

A. tension
B. compression
C. thrust
D. spread

364. Which of the following are required to be included in truss design drawings.

A. location of all joints
B. nailing schedule
C. web bracing live load
D. web bracing dead load

365. Foam plastic trim defined as picture molds, chair rails, baseboards, handrails, ceiling beams, door trim and window trim may be installed, provided

_____.

A. The minimum density is 20 pounds per cubic foot
B. The maximum thickness of the trim is 0.5 inch and the maximum width is 8 inches
C. The trim constitutes no more than 10 percent of the area of any wall or ceiling
D. The flame-spread rating does not exceed 75
E. all of the above conditions must be present

366. Fasteners for pressure preservative and fire-retardant-treated wood may be _____ diameter or greater steel bolts.

A. 1/2 inch
B. 1 inch
C. 1 1/2 inch
D. 2 inch

367. What is the required ventilation area in square feet for a crawl space under a 2400 square foot dwelling. There is no Class 1 vapor retarder material being used.

A. 10
B. 12
C. 16
D. 24

368. For onsite construction, from time to time the building official, upon notification from the _____, shall make or cause to be made any necessary inspections and shall either approve that portion of the construction as completed or shall notify the permit holder or his or her agent wherein the same fails to comply with this code.

    A. owner
    B. contractor
    C. permit holder or his agent
    D. none of the above

369. Wood studwalls shall be capped with a double top plate installed to provide overlapping at corners and intersections with bearing partitions with the end joints in top plates offset at least _____ inches

    A. 12
    B. 24
    C. 36
    D. 48

370. The minimum clear width of the stairway at and below the handrail height, including treads and landings, shall not be less than _____ inches where a handrail is installed on one side and _____ inches where handrails are provided on both sides. Exceptions ignored.

    A. 36,   30
    B. 34,   28
    C. 31.5,   27
    D. 27,   27

371. Where emergency escape and rescue openings are provided in they shall have a sill height of not more than _____ inches above the floor

    A. 36
    B. 44
    C. 48
    D. 60

372.   The provisions of this code _____ be deemed to nullify any provisions of local, state or federal law.

    A. shall not
    B. shall

373.   If the handrail is not circular it shall have a perimeter dimension of at least _____ inches and not greater than _____ inches with a maximum cross section of dimension of _____ inches.

    A. 4, 61/4, 21/4
    B. 4, 5, 21/4
    C. 4, 61/4, 4
    D. 4, 61/4, 3

374.   Foam plastic board of not more than 1/2-inch thickness may be used as siding backer board when separated from interior spaces by not less than 2 inches of mineral fiber insulation or 1/2-inch gypsum wallboard or installed over existing exterior wall finish in conjunction with re-siding, providing the plastic board does not have a potential heat of more than Btu per square foot when tested in accordance with NFPA 259, but only with other provisions satisfied as well.

    A. 1,000
    B. 1,500
    C. 2,000
    D. 3,000

375.   What is the fastener requirement for the wood ceiling joists not attached to parallel rafter, laps over partitions, face nailed.

    A. 3-10d
    B. 3-16d
    C. 3-8d
    D. 4-16d

376. The minimum size of habitable rooms shall be a floor area of not less than _____ square feet.

   A. 50
   B. 120
   C. 70
   D. 90

377. An existing roof has one roofing application, which of the following is true.

   A. All existing roofing must be always be removed before a new installation layer can be applied
   B. A new installation layer of roofing may sometimes be applied over the existing.
   C. Only asphalt shingles can be applied over the existing layer
   D. none of the above

378. When the winter design temperature is below 60°F, every dwelling unit shall be provided with heating facilities capable of maintaining a minimum room temperature of _____ at a point _____ feet above the floor and _____ feet from exterior walls in all habitable rooms at the design temperature.

   A. 60°F, 4, 3
   B. 70°F, 5,3
   C. 68°F, 3, 2
   D. 68°F, 6, 4

379. For residential subdivisions where all dwellings are equipped throughout with an automatic sprinkler systems installed in accordance with Section P2904, the fire separation distance for nonrated exterior walls and rated projections shall be permitted to be reduced to _____ feet, and unlimited unprotected openings and penetrations shall be permitted, where the adjoining lot provides an open setback yard that is _____ feet or more in width on the opposite side of the property line.

   A. 2, 6
   B. 3, 8
   C. 0, 6
   D. 0, 0

380. What is the maximum allowable span for #1 Spruce-pine-fir 2X6 floor joist space 19.2 inches OC with a live load of 30 psf and a dead load of 10 psf, in residential sleeping areas.

A. 10 feet 8 inches
B. 9 feet 3 inches
C. 9 feet 6 inches
D. 9 feet 8 inches

381. What is the minimum aggregate ratio (measured in damp, loose conditions) for mortar type cement.

A. not less than 21/4 and not more than 3 times the sum of separate volumes of lime, if used, and cement
B. not less than 1 and not more than 3 times the sum of separate volumes of lime, if used, and cement
C. not less than 21/4 and not more than 4 times the sum of separate volumes of lime, if used, and cement
D. non of the above

382. The area of floor used for parking of automobiles or other vehicles shall be _____.

A. sloped to facilitate the movement of liquids to a drain or toward the main vehicle entry doorway
B. level and a minimum of 8" above the road surface
C. a minimum of 6" wire reinforced concrete
D. none of the above

383. Within any flight of stairs, the greatest winder tread depth at the walk line shall not exceed the smallest by more than _____ inch(es).

A. 3/8
B. 1/2
C. 4
D. 6

384. What is the minimum wall thickness in inches for a plain masonry foundation wall with a height of 7 feet with a unbalanced backfill height of 7 feet constructed in sandy gravel soil.

    A. 6 solid
    B. 8
    C. 10
    D. 12

Section 2

Timed Exams

Each exam has 60 Questions, there are 6 exams with the questions in random order.
Time yourself, allow yourself 2 hours to complete each exam. This will develop your time management skills as well as giving you review knowledge and lookup practice.

Timed Exam 1   2 Hours to Complete

Timed Exam 1 - 1. If any concealed trap, drain pipe, water, soil, waste or vent pipe becomes defective and it becomes necessary to remove and replace the same with new material, such work shall be considered as

_____.

    A. old work no permit is needed
    B. new work and a permit shall be obtained
    C. existing work
    D. none of the above

Timed Exam 1 - 2. What is minimum specified compressive strength of concrete in psi for basement walls, foundation walls, exterior walls and other vertical concrete work exposed to the weather with moderate weathering potential.

    A. 1500
    B. 2000
    C. 3000
    D. 3500

Timed Exam 1 - 3. _____ glazing in railings regardless of area or height above a walking surface are hazardous locations. Included are structural baluster panels and nonstructural infill panels.

    A. All
    B. 30 inch high
    C. 24 inch high
    D. 60 inch high

Timed Exam 1 - 4. The finished grade of under floor surface may be located at the bottom of the footings, where there is evidence that the groundwater table can rise to within _____ inches of the finished floor at the building perimeter or where there is evidence that the surface water does not readily drain from the building site, the grade in the under floor space shall be as high as the outside finished grade, unless an approved drainage system is provided.

    A. 4
    B. 6
    C. 8
    D. 12

Timed Exam 1 - 5.   Habitable space, hallways, bathrooms, toilet rooms, laundry rooms and portions of basements containing these spaces shall have a ceiling height of not less than _____ feet

    A. 6.8
    B. 6
    C. 7
    D. 7.2

Timed Exam 1 - 6.   The opening between adjacent treads is not limited on stairs with a total rise of _____ inches or less.

    A. 15
    B. 24
    C. 30
    D. 42

Timed Exam 1 - 7.   Hollow concrete piers shall be capped with _____ of solid masonry or concrete, a masonry cap block, or shall have cavities of the top course filled with concrete or grout.

    A. 4 inches (102 mm)
    B. 6 inches (152 mm)
    C. 8 inches (203 mm)
    D. 12 inches (102 mm)

Timed Exam 1 - 8.   Where lighting outlets are installed in interior stairways, there shall be a wall switch at each floor level to control the lighting outlet where the stairway has _____ or more risers.

    A. 3
    B. 4
    C. 5
    D. 6

Timed Exam 1 - 9.   Where work requiring a permit occurs in existing dwellings that have attached garages or in existing dwellings within which _____ exist, carbon monoxide alarms shall be provided.

A. baseboard resistance heating appliances
B. refrigerator freezers
C. fuel-fired appliances
D. all of these

Timed Exam 1 - 10. All emergency escape and rescue openings shall have a minimum net clear opening width of _____ inches.

A. 18
B. 20
C. 24
D. 30

Timed Exam 1 - 11. An application for a permit for any proposed work shall be deemed to have been abandoned _____ days after the date of filing, unless such application has been pursued in good faith or a permit has been issued.

A. 45
B. 90
C. 180
D. 360

Timed Exam 1 - 12. Habitable rooms shall not be less than _____ feet in any horizontal dimension.

A. 6
B. 7
C. 8
D. 10

Timed Exam 1 - 13. Used materials, equipment and devices

_____.

    A. shall not be reused under any circumstance in new construction
    B. shall be reused if the general contractor will accept liability for material performance failure.
    C. shall not be reused unless approved by the building official
    D. none of the above

Timed Exam 1 - 14. What is the minimum wall thickness in inches for a plain masonry foundation wall with a height of 9 feet with a unbalanced backfill height of 8 feet constructed in sand soil.

    A. 6
    B. 8
    C. 12
    D. 12 solid

Timed Exam 1 - 15. There shall be a floor or landing _____ of each exterior door. Exceptions ignored.

    A. on the inside
    B. on the outside
    C. on either the inside or outside
    D. on each side

Timed Exam 1 - 16. What is the fastener requirement for the roof rafters to ridge, valley or hip rafters face nailed when using 16d nails.

    A. 2-16d
    B. 3-8d
    C. 3-16d
    D. 4-10d

Timed Exam 1 - 17. Where enforcement of a code provision would violate the conditions of the listing of the equipment or appliance, appliance, the

_____.

A. building official shall decide which provision shall apply.
B. the board of review shall decide which provision shall apply.
C. conditions of the listing and manufacturer's instructions shall apply
D. None of the above

Timed Exam 1 - 18. Emergency escape and rescue openings with a finished sill height below the adjacent ground elevation must be provided with a

_____.

A. handrail
B. exit sign
C. window well
D. emergency lighting unit

Timed Exam 1 - 19. Stairways shall not be less than _____ inches in clear width at all points above the permitted handrail height and below the required headroom height.

A. 30
B. 32
C. 36
D. 44

Timed Exam 1 - 20. Studs shall be continuous from support at the sole plate to a support at the top plate to resist loads perpendicular to the wall. The support shall be a foundation or floor, ceiling or roof diaphragm or shall be designed in accordance with _____.

A. local traditional design
B. maximum engineering values
C. accepted engineering practice
D. non of the above

Timed Exam 1 - 21. The required quality mark on each piece of pressure preservatively treated lumber or plywood shall contain which of the following information.

      A. Identification of the treating plant, type of preservative, the minimum preservative retention end use for which the product was treated
      B. Standard to which the product was treated, identity of the approved inspection agency
      C. identity of the approved inspection agency, the designation "Dry", if applicable.
      D. all of the above

Timed Exam 1 - 22. What is the weathering probability factor for the state of Wisconsin.

      A. Severe
      B. Moderate
      C. Negligible
      D. Extremely Severe

Timed Exam 1 - 23. Truss design drawings, shall be provided to the building official and approved _____.

      A. prior to installation
      B. at the job site
      C. after installation is completed
      D. none of the above

Timed Exam 1 - 24. Submittal documents consisting of construction documents, and other data shall be submitted in two or more sets with each application for a permit. The construction documents shall be prepared by a _____ where required by the statutes of the jurisdiction in which the project is to be constructed. Where special conditions exist, the building official is authorized to require additional construction documents to be prepared by a _____.

A. licensed architect, licensed architect
B. licensed engineer, licensed engineer
C. registered design professional, registered design professional
D. any of these

Timed Exam 1 - 25. Corrosion-resistant flashing at the base of an opening that is integrated into the building exterior wall to direct water to the exterior and is premanufactured, fabricated, formed or applied at the job site.

A. PAN FLASHING.
B. WINDOW WELL FLASHING
C. CORBLING FLASHING
D. DIVERSION FLASHING

Timed Exam 1 - 26. For solid masonry units, solid grouted hollow units, or hollow units in anchored masonry veneer, wall ties shall be embedded in mortar bed at least _____.

A. 1 inch (25.4 mm)
B. 2 inches (38 mm)
C. 11/2 inches (50.8 mm)
D. 3 inches (76.2mm)

Timed Exam 1 - 27. Untreated wood may be used where

_____.

A. painted properly
B. partial submerged in fresh water
C. entirely below groundwater level or continuously submerged in fresh water
D. none of the above

Timed Exam 1 - 28. Joists exceeding a nominal _____ shall be supported laterally by solid blocking, diagonal bridging (wood or metal), or a continuous 1-inch-by-3-inch strip nailed across the bottom of joists perpendicular to joists at intervals not exceeding 8 feet. Exceptions ignored.

A. 2 x 12
B. 2 x 10
C. 2 x 8
D. 2 x 6

Timed Exam 1 - 29. Where a stairway of _____ risers is located on the exterior side of a door, other than the required exit door, a landing is not required for the exterior side of the door.

  A. two
  B. two or fewer
  C. three
  D. two or fewer

Timed Exam 1 - 30. Openings for required guards on the sides of stair treads shall not allow a sphere _____ inches to pass through.

  A. 4
  B. 4 3/8
  C. 6
  D. 6 3/8

Timed Exam 1 - 31. Marathon County Wisconsin is in which energy conservation climate zone.

  A. 3A
  B. 4B
  C. 6A
  D. 7

Timed Exam 1 - 32. What is the maximum ceiling joist span for #2 Hem-fir 2X8 spaced 12 inches OC, with a live load of 10 PSF and a dead load of 5 PSF in an uninhabitable attics without storage.

  A. 10-3
  B. 15-10
  C. 18-2
  D. 24-0

Timed Exam 1 - 33. When there is usable space both above and below the concealed space of a floor/ceiling assembly, draftstops shall be installed so that the area of the concealed space does not exceed _____ square feet.

A. 750
B. 1,000
C. 1,500
D. 2,000

Timed Exam 1 - 34. Slabs on ground with turned down footings shall have a minimum of one _____ at the top and the bottom of the footing. Exceptions ignored.

A. No. 3 bar
B. No. 4 bar
C. No. 5 bar
D. No. 6 bar

Timed Exam 1 - 35. What is the maximum rafter span for #1 S-P-F 2X12 spaced 16 inches OC with a ground snow load of 30 PSF and a dead load of 20 PSF with the ceiling not attached to the rafters.

A. 16-6
B. 13-6
C. 23-6
D. 19-2

Timed Exam 1 - 36. Dwelling units in two-family dwellings shall be separated from each other by wall and/or floor assemblies having not less than _____ hour fire-resistance rating. Exceptions ignored.

A. 1/3
B. 1/2
C. 1
D. 2

Timed Exam 1 - 37. Foundation cripple walls shall be framed of studs not less in size than the studding above and when exceeding _____ feet in height, such walls shall be framed of studs having the size required for an additional story.

  A. 3
  B. 4
  C. 5
  D. 6

Timed Exam 1 - 38. The minimum width for concrete and masonry footings for a 1 story 8-inch solid or fully grouted masonry construction dwelling where the soil load bearing value is 1500 psf is _____ inches.

  A. 12
  B. 16
  C. 32
  D. 42

Timed Exam 1 - 39. Foam plastic, except where otherwise noted, shall be separated from the interior of a building by minimum _____ inch gypsum board or an approved finish material.

  A. 3/8
  B. 1/2
  C. 5/8
  D. 3/4

Timed Exam 1 - 40. Basic wind speed is defined as a _____ second gust speed at 33 feet above the ground in wind exposure C .

  A. one
  B. three
  C. ten
  D. sixty

Timed Exam 1 - 41. Joists framing from opposite sides over a bearing support shall lap a minimum of _____ inches and shall be nailed together with a minimum _____ 10d face nails.

A. 3, 1
B. 4, 2
C. 3, 3
D. 4, 2

Timed Exam 1 - 42. Openings in doors through which a _____ inch sphere is unable to pass is not considered a hazardous location with respect to glazing.

A. 3
B. 6
C. 9
D. 12

Timed Exam 1 - 43. Floor cantilevers in cold-formed steel framing shall not exceed _____ inches.

A. 12
B. 24
C. 36
D. 48

Timed Exam 1 - 44. _____ as required by this code, shall be available on the job site at the time of inspection.

A. General Contractors license
B. A list of contractors & sub-contractors
C. Inspection certificates
D. Manufacturer's installation instructions

Timed Exam 1 - 45. Handrail height, measured above the finished surface of the ramp slope, shall be not less than _____ inches and not more than _____ inches.

A. 30, 42
B. 34, 40
C. 36, 42
D. 34, 38

116

Timed Exam 1 - 46. The floor or landing at the exit door required by code shall not be more than _____ inches lower than the top of the threshold. Exceptions ignored.

    A. .25
    B. .75
    C. 1.5
    D. 7.75

Timed Exam 1 - 47. The building official is hereby authorized and directed to enforce the provisions of this code and he shall have the authority to _____ of this code and to adopt policies and procedures in order to clarify the application of its provisions.

    A. render interpretations
    B. modify the articles
    C. wave sections in the enforcement
    D. none of the above

Timed Exam 1 - 48. The minimum horizontal area of the window well used as a emergency escape and rescue shall be _____ square feet, with a minimum horizontal projection and width of 36 inches.

    A. 6
    B. 9
    C. 12
    D. 15

Timed Exam 1 - 49. What is the maximum allowable span for cold-formed steel joists size 1200S162-54 loaded with a live load of 30 PSF and spaced 16 inches OC.

    A. 23'- 4"
    B. 19'-7"
    C. 21'-3"
    D. 17'-6"

Timed Exam 1 - 50. For the purpose of determining light and ventilation requirements, any room shall be considered as a portion of an adjoining room when at least 1/2 of the area of the common wall is open and unobstructed and provides an opening of not less than 1/10 of the floor area of the interior room but not less than _____ square feet.

    A. 25
    B. 50
    C. 75
    D. 100

Timed Exam 1 - 51. A single flat 2X4 member may be used as a header in interior or exterior nonbearing walls for openings up to _____ feet in width if the vertical distance to the parallel nailing surface above is not more than _____ inches.

    A. 4, 12
    B. 8, 24
    C. 6, 18
    D. 5, 24

Timed Exam 1 - 52. For new construction, an approved _____ alarm shall be installed outside of each separate sleeping area in the immediate vicinity of the bedrooms in dwelling units within which fuel-fired appliances are installed and in dwelling units that have attached garages.

    A. carbon dioxide
    B. carbon monoxide
    C. greenhouse gas
    D. methane gas

Timed Exam 1 - 53. What is the presumed load bearing value in pounds per square foot of crystalline bedrock.

    A. 1,500
    B. 2,000
    C. 4,000
    D. 12,000

Timed Exam 1 - 54. The ends of each rafter or ceiling joist shall have not less than _____ inches of bearing on wood or metal and not less than _____ inches on masonry or concrete.

A. 11/2, 3   1½,3 NoT 11/2
B. 2, 4
C. 2, 3
D. 11/2, 4

Timed Exam 1 - 55. Foam-filled doors _____ from the requirements of Section R314.1.

A. are exempt
B. are included

Timed Exam 1 - 56. The minimum width for concrete and masonry footings for a 3 story 8-inch solid or fully grouted masonry construction dwelling where the soil load bearing value is 1500 psf is _____ inches.

A. 12
B. 21
C. 29
D. 42

Timed Exam 1 - 57. Which of the following does not require a permit.

A. Retaining walls that are not over 4 feet in height measured from the bottom of the footing to the top of the wall, unless supporting a surcharge.
B. Water tanks supported directly upon grade if the capacity does not exceed 5,000 gallons and the ratio of height to diameter or width does not exceed 2 to 1.
C. Sidewalks and driveways.
D. Painting, papering, tiling, carpeting, cabinets, counter tops and similar finish work.
E. all of the above

Timed Exam 1 - 58. What is the presumed load bearing value in pounds per square foot of sedimentary and foliated rock.

    A. 1,500
    B. 2,000
    C. 4,000
    D. 12,000

Timed Exam 1 - 59. Within crawlspaces where entry is made only for service of utilities, foam plastics shall be protected against ignition by

_____,

    A. 11/2-inch-thick mineral fiber insulation or 1/4-inch hardboard
    B. 1/4-inchthick wood structural panels or 3/8-inch gypsum board
    C. 3/8-inch particleboard, or corrosion-resistant steel having a base metal thick-ness of 0.016 inch
    D. any or all of the above

Timed Exam 1 - 60. Every landing where a stairway has a straight run shall have a minimum dimension of _____ measured in the direction of travel.

    A. 36 inches
    B. 32 inches
    C. 44 inches
    D. non of the above

Timed Exam 2   2 Hours to Complete

Timed Exam 2 - 1.   What is the maximum span for a header constructed of 3 2X8s douglas fir-larch a building 28 feet wide and supporting the two floors.

    A. 4 feet 5 inches
    B. 6 feet 7 inches
    C. 3 feet 6 inches
    D. 6 feet 3 inches

5' 2

Timed Exam 2 - 2.   The building official is authorized to make all of the required inspections, or the building official shall have the authority to

_____.

    A. receive signed affidavits by the owner or contractor
    B. accept reports of inspection by approved agencies or individuals
    C. wave any and all inspections
    D. none of the above

Timed Exam 2 - 3.   A one story detached accessory structures with an area of less than _____ square feet does not require a permit.

    A. 100
    B. 200
    C. 300
    D. 400

Timed Exam 2 - 4.   The greatest tread depth within any flight of stairs shall not exceed the smallest by more than _____ inch.

    A. .25
    B. 3/8
    C. .375
    D. B or C

Timed Exam 2 - 5. The concentration, rate of application and treatment method of the termiticide shall be in strict compliance with _____.

      A. 5 lbs. per 100 sq ft
      B. 10 lbs. per 100 sq ft
      C. 20 lbs. per 100 sq ft
      D. the termiticide label

Timed Exam 2 - 6. A porous layer of gravel, crushed stone or coarse sand shall be placed to a minimum thickness of _____ inches under the basement floor. Provision shall be made for automatic draining of this layer and the gravel or crushed stone wall footings.

      A. 2
      B. 3
      C. 4
      D. 6

Timed Exam 2 - 7. A stud may be bored to a diameter not exceeding _____ percent of its width, provided that such studs located in exterior walls or bearing partitions are and are bored over _____ percent that they be doubled and that not more than two successive studs are bored.

      A. 25, 10
      B. 40, 35
      C. 60, 40
      D. 75, 60

Timed Exam 2 - 8. A roof covering composed of flat-plate photovoltaic modules fabricated into shingles.

      A. GREEN ENERGY SHINGLES
      B. ELECTRIC SOLAR BLANKET
      C. LOW ENERGY MODULES
      D. PHOTOVOLTAIC MODULES/SHINGLES

Timed Exam 2 - 9. A stair nosing is not required where the tread depth is a minimum of _____ inches.

    A. 10
    B. 11
    C. 12
    D. 11.5

Timed Exam 2 - 10. All habitable rooms shall be provided with aggregate glazing area of not less than percent of the floor area of such rooms. Natural ventilation shall be through windows, doors, Exceptions ignored.

    A. 4
    B. 6
    C. 8
    D. 10

Timed Exam 2 - 11. Asphalt shingles shall only be used on roof slopes of _____ units vertical in 12 units horizontal or greater.

    A. 2
    B. 3
    C. 4
    D. 5

Timed Exam 2 - 12. Handrails shall be provided on at least one side of each continuous run of treads or flight with _____ or more risers.

    A. two
    B. three
    C. four
    D. six

Timed Exam 2 - 13. What is the fastener requirement for the wood ceiling joists to plate, toe nailed.

    A. 2-10d
    B. 3-10d
    C. 8-16d
    D. 3-8d

Timed Exam 2 - 14. Wood shingles shall be installed on slopes of three units vertical in _____ percent slope or greater.

      A. 10
      B. 20
      C. 25
      D. 40

Timed Exam 2 - 15. The maximum total deflection of structural members that support glass unit masonry shall not exceed _____.

      A. l/300
      B. l/500
      C. l/600
      D. l/160

Timed Exam 2 - 16. Smoke alarms shall be installed in which of the following locations.
      A. In each sleeping room
      B. Outside each separate sleeping area in the immediate vicinity of the bedrooms
      C. On each additional story of the dwelling, including basements but not including crawl spaces and uninhabitable attics
      D. all of the above

Timed Exam 2 - 17. Fasteners for pressure preservative and fire-retardant-treated wood shall be _____.

      A. steel or iron
      B. screws only
      C. hot-dipped galvanized steel, stainless steel, silicon bronze or copper.
      D. stainless steel only

Timed Exam 2 - 18. Portions of a room with a sloping ceiling measuring less than _____ feet or a furred ceiling measuring less than _____ feet from the finished floor to the finished ceiling shall not be considered as contributing to the minimum required habitable area for that room.

      A. 4, 8
      B. 5, 7
      C. 4, 7
      D. 3, 6

Timed Exam 2 - 19. What are the required steel reinforcement rods for an 8 inch thick masonry foundation wall with a height of 6 feet 8 inches with an unbalanced backfill height of 5 feet constructed in sandy gravel soil.

    A. #3 at 48" o.c.
    B. #4 at 48" o.c.
    C. #4 at 60" o.c.
    D. #4 at 72" o.c.

Timed Exam 2 - 20. All exterior footings shall be placed at least _____ inches below the undisturbed ground surface.

    A. 12
    B. 16
    C. 20
    D. 24

Timed Exam 2 - 21. The building official shall receive applications, review construction documents and issue permits for the erection and alteration of buildings and structures, inspect the premises for which such permits have been issued and _____.

    A. reject any provision of this code he sees fit
    B. enforce compliance with the provisions of this code
    C. add any articles he feels the code is lacking
    D. all of the above

Timed Exam 2 - 22. All vertical joints of panel sheathing shall occur over, and be fastened to, common studs. Horizontal joints in braced wall panels shall occur over, and be fastened to, common blocking of a minimum _____ thickness.

    A. 1 1/2 inch (38 mm)
    B. 2 inch (50.8 mm)
    C. 1 inch (25.4 mm)
    D. 3/4 inch (19.0 mm)

Timed Exam 2 - 23. What is the fastener requirement for the blocking between wood joists or rafters to top plate, toe nail.

A. 3-8d
B. 4-8d
C. 3-10d
D. 4-10d

Timed Exam 2 - 24. An artificial light source is not required at the top and bottom landing, provided an artificial light source is located

_____.

A. adjacent to the stairway
B. at the beginning and end
C. directly over each stairway section
D. none of the above

Timed Exam 2 - 25. All smoke alarms shall be installed in accordance with the provisions of this code and the household fire warning equipment provisions of

_____.

A. NFPA 13
B. IRC 72
C. NFPA 72
D. none of the above

Timed Exam 2 - 26. The ends of each joist, beam or girder shall have not less than _____ inches of bearing on metal. Exceptions ignored

A. 1.5
B. 2
C. 3
D. 4

Timed Exam 2 - 27. Openings from a private garage directly into a room used for sleeping purposes _____.

   A. must be protected by a minimum 20 minute fire rated covering.
   B. must have a 1- 3/8 inch self closing door with a 20 minute fire rating.
   C. are limited to single leaf swinging doors with 20 minute fire rating.
   D. shall not be permitted

Timed Exam 2 - 28. A three story dwelling is in a area that has a basic wind speed of 70 mph. The top floor of the structure uses the LIB method of bracing to resist the lateral wind forces. The Southern exterior braced wall line on this top floor has a braced wall line spacing of 30 feet. What is the minimum total length in feet of braced wall panels required along this braced wall line?

   A. 4.5
   B. 8.5
   C. 12
   D. 15.5

Timed Exam 2 - 29. Handrails shall be permitted to be interrupted by a newel post _____.

   A. at the turn
   B. only
   C. if the turn is more than 90 degrees
   D. none of the above

Timed Exam 2 - 30. Wood foundation basements shall be drained and _____ in accordance with Sections R405 and R406, respectively.

   A. dampproofed
   B. waterproofed
   C. rainproofed
   D. none of the above

Timed Exam 2 - 31. For roof slopes from two units vertical in 12 units horizontal up to _____ units vertical in 12 units horizontal, double underlayment application is required in accordance with Section R905.2.7.

A. 3
B. 4
C. 5
D. 6

Timed Exam 2 - 32. What is the maximum stud spacing for nominal panel thickness of 7/16 inch wood structural panel wall sheathing used to resist wind pressures.

A. 16
B. 19.2
C. 24
D. 32

Timed Exam 2 - 33. Handrails with a circular cross section shall have an outside diameter of at least _____ inches and not greater than _____ inches .

A. 13/4, 2
B. 11/4, 2 1/2
C. 11/4, 2
D. 1, 2 1/4

Timed Exam 2 - 34. A comparative measure, expressed as a dimensionless number, derived from measurements of smoke obscuration versus time for a material tested in accordance with ASTM E 84 or UL 723.

A. FLAME TO SMOKE RATIO INDEX
B. SMOKE-DEVELOPED INDEX
C. TOXIC GAS INDEX
D. OBSURATION INDEX

Timed Exam 2 - 35. The wood sole plate at exterior walls on monolithic slabs and wood sill plate shall be anchored to the foundation with anchor bolts spaced a maximum of _____ feet on center.

A. 2
B. 4
C. 6
D. 8

Timed Exam 2 - 36. Any stud may be bored or drilled, provided that the diameter of the resulting hole is no greater than _____ percent of the stud width, the edge of the hole is no closer than 5/8 inch to the edge of the stud, and the hole is not located in the same section as a cut or notch. Exceptions ignored.

A. 25
B. 40
C. 50
D. 60

Timed Exam 2 - 37. An automatic residential fire sprinkler system shall not be required when additions or alterations are made to _____ townhouses that do not have an automatic residential fire sprinkler system installed.

A. new single story
B. new slab on grade
C. existing
D. none of these

Timed Exam 2 - 38. Winder stairway treads shall have a minimum tread depth of _____ inches measured between the vertical planes of the foremost projection of adjacent treads at the intersections with the walkline.

A. 10
B. 9
C. 8
D. 9.5

Timed Exam 2 - 39. What is the maximum span for a header constructed of 2 2X6s southern pine in building 28 feet wide and supporting the roof and ceiling. The ground snow load is 50 psf.

    A. 3 feet 11 inches
    B. 4 feet 1 inches
    C. 3 feet 6 inches
    D. 4 feet 8 inches

Timed Exam 2 - 40. Before issuing a permit, the building official _____ or cause to be examined buildings, structures and sites for which an application has been filed.

    A. is authorized to examine
    B. must examine
    C. shall examine
    D. no authority to examine

Timed Exam 2 - 41. A _____ inch thick base course consisting of clean graded sand, gravel, crushed stone or crushed blast-furnace slag passing a 2 inch sieve shall be placed on the prepared subgrade when the slab is below grade. Exceptions ignored.

    A. 2
    B. 3
    C. 4
    D. 5

Timed Exam 2 - 42. Garage floor surfaces shall be of approved _____ material.

    A. noncombustible
    B. concrete
    C. asphalt or concrete
    D. cement

Timed Exam 2 - 43. Beveling of stair nosing shall not exceed _____ inch.

    A. 3/8
    B. 1/2
    C. 3/4
    D. 1/4

Timed Exam 2 - 44. The construction documents submitted with the application for permit shall be accompanied by a _____ showing the size and location of new construction and existing structures on the site and distances from lot lines.

    A. layout sketch
    B. plot rendering
    C. site plan
    D. none of these

Timed Exam 2 - 45. A composite of wood strand elements with wood fibers primarily oriented along the length of the member, where the least dimension of the wood strand elements is 0.10 inch (2.54 mm) or less and their average lengths are a minimum of 75 times and less than 150 times the least dimension of the wood strand elements.

    A. Laminated strand lumber (LSL)
    B. Parallel strand lumber (PSL)
    C. Oriented strand lumber (OSL)
    D. Laminated veneer lumber (LVL)

Timed Exam 2 - 46. Where a masonry or metal rain cap is installed on a masonry chimney, the net free area under the cap shall not be less than _____ the net free area of the outlet of the chimney flue it serves.

    A. two times
    B. three times
    C. four times
    D. ten times
    E. none of these

Timed Exam 2 - 47. Where there is a conflict between a general requirement and a specific requirement, the _____ requirement shall be applicable.

   A. specific
   B. general
   C. most general
   D. least specific

Timed Exam 2 - 48. What is minimum specified compressive strength of concrete in psi for porches, carport slabs and steps exposed to the weather, and garage floor slabs with severe weathering potential.

   A. 1500
   B. 2000
   C. 2500
   D. 3500

Timed Exam 2 - 49. Which type of glazing my not be used in a skylight.

   A. Fully tempered glass.
   B. Heat strengthened glass.
   C. Double strength glass.
   D. Wired glass.

Timed Exam 2 - 50. All emergency escape and rescue openings shall have a minimum net clear opening of _____ square feet. Exceptions ignored.

   A. 3.2
   B. 9
   C. 5.7
   D. 7.5

Timed Exam 2 - 51. The fire-resistance-rated wall or assembly separating townhouses for townhouses shall be continuous from the foundation to the underside of the roof sheathing, deck or slab and shall extend the full length of the _____ including walls extending through and separating attached accessory structures.

A. exterior walls
B. wall or assembly
C. joint wall
D. non of the above

Timed Exam 2 - 52. All foam plastic or foam plastic cores used as a component in manufactured assemblies used in building construction shall have a flame-spread rating of not more than _____ and shall have a smoke-developed rating of not more than _____. Exceptions ignored.

    A. 75, 450
    B. 450, 75
    C. 100, 350
    D. 350, 100

Timed Exam 2 - 53. When fire sprinklers are installed in a garage, is and overhead garage door considered to be an obstruction with respect to placement of the sprinkler heads?

    A. Yes
    B. No
    C. Overhead doors can not be used.
    D. Extra sprinkler heads must be used to cover the areas obstructed by the overhead door when open.

Timed Exam 2 - 54. Cleanout openings shall be provided within _____ inches of the base of each flue within every masonry chimney.

    A. 3
    B. 6
    C. 12
    D. 24

Timed Exam 2 - 55. The minimum width for concrete and masonry footings for a 2 story 4-inch brick veneer over light frame or 8-inch hollow concrete masonry construction dwelling where the soil load bearing value is 2000 psf is _____ inches.

    A. 12
    B. 16
    C. 21
    D. 24

Timed Exam 2 - 56. What is the maximum span for sanded plywood combination subfloor underlayment of Species Group 2 if the plywood is 3/4 inch thick.

    A. 16
    B. 20
    C. 24
    D. 32

Timed Exam 2 - 57. An exterior wall element is required to be fire-resistance rated, there is another structure less than 5 feet of the fire-resistance rated wall. Is this a violation of the code?

    A. Yes
    B. No
    C. Code does not apply here.
    D. not enough information to answer

Timed Exam 2 - 58. The total net free ventilating area of an attic shall not be less than 1 to _____ of the area of the space. Exceptions ignored.

    A. 50
    B. 100
    C. 150
    D. 200

Timed Exam 2 - 59. Emergency escape and rescue openings shall be operational from the inside of the room _____.

    A. keys, tools or special knowledge
    B. with three movements of the hand or less
    C. with outward force disengagement hardware
    D. all of the above

Timed Exam 2 - 60. What are the required steel reinforcement rods for an 10 inch thick foundation wall with a height of 9 feet with a unbalanced backfill height of 8 feet constructed in SC soil.

        A. #4 at 24" o.c.
        B. #4 at 48" o.c.
        C. #5 at 56" o.c.
        D. #6 at 40" o.c.

Timed Exam 3   2 Hours to Complete

Timed Exam 3 - 1.   What is the maximum allowable span for #1 Spruce-pine-fir 2X6 floor joist space 19.2 inches OC with a live load of 40 psf and a dead load of 10 psf, in residential living areas..

    A. 9 feet 8 inches
    B. 8 feet 9 inches
    C. 10 feet 6 inches
    D. 7 feet 8 inches

Timed Exam 3 - 2.   What is the minimum wall thickness in inches for a plain masonry foundation wall with a height of 7 feet with a unbalanced backfill height of 4 feet constructed in sandy clay soil.

    A. 5
    B. 6
    C. 7
    D. 8

Timed Exam 3 - 3.   Type GW soil is a Group _____ soil group member.

    A. I
    B. II
    C. III
    D. IV

Timed Exam 3 - 4.   The rough-framed opening for attic access shall not be less than _____ inches and shall be located in a hallway or other readily accessible location.

    A. 18X22
    B. 22X30
    C. 24X30
    D. 18X30

Timed Exam 3 - 5.   Concrete slab-on-ground floors shall be a minimum _____ inches thick.

A. 4.5
B. 4
C. 3
D. 3.5

Timed Exam 3 - 6. Piping or ductwork placed in or partly in an exterior wall or interior load-bearing wall, necessitating cutting, drilling or notching of the top plate by more than 50 percent of its width, a galvanized metal tie of not less than _____ inches thick and 11/2 inches wide shall be fastened to each plate across and to each side of the opening with not less than _____ 10d nails having a minimum length of 11/2 inches (38 mm) at each side or equivalent.

A. 0.054, 8
B. 0.25, 8
C. 0.054, 6
D. 0.01, 4

Timed Exam 3 - 7. Handrails adjacent to a wall shall have a space of not less than _____ inch between the wall and the handrails.

A. 1- /2
B. 1-1/4
C. 2
D. 1

Timed Exam 3 - 8. A flight of stairs shall not have a vertical rise greater than _____ between floor levels or landings.

A. 13 steps
B. 12 feet
C. 13 feet
D. 12 steps

Timed Exam 3 - 9. All emergency escape and rescue openings shall have a minimum net clear opening height of _____ inches.

A. 18
B. 24
C. 30
D. 36

Timed Exam 3 - 10. With regard to wood floor framing, blocking shall be a minimum of utility grade lumber. Subflooring may be a minimum of utility grade lumber or _____ common grade boards.

> A. No. 1
> B. No. 2
> C. No. 3
> D. No. 4

Timed Exam 3 - 11. A handrail shall be provided on at least one side of all ramps exceeding a slope of one unit vertical in _____ units horizontal.

> A. 6
> B. 8
> C. 10
> D. 12

Timed Exam 3 - 12. Notches in solid lumber joists, rafters and beams shall not exceed _____ of the depth of the member, shall not be longer than one-third of the depth of the member and shall not be located in the middle one-third of the span.

> A. one-third
> B. one-fourth
> C. one-sixth
> D. one-fifth

Timed Exam 3 - 13. Every permit issued shall become invalid unless the work authorized by such permit is commenced within _____ days after its issuance, or if the work authorized by such permit is suspended or abandoned for a period of _____ days after the time the work is commenced.

> A. 45, 90
> B. 90, 180
> C. 180, 180
> D. 365, 180

Timed Exam 3 - 14. When the header joist span exceeds _____ feet, the trimmer joists and the header joist shall be doubled and of sufficient cross section to support the floor joists framing into the header.

    A. 3
    B. 4
    C. 5
    D. 6

Timed Exam 3 - 15. On a wall that required braced wall line, if there is a diagonal wall section and the section is longer than _____ feet, then it must be treated as a separate braced wall line.

    A. 4
    B. 6
    C. 8
    D. 12

Timed Exam 3 - 16. The ends of each joist, beam or girder shall have not less than _____ inches of bearing on wood or metal. Exceptions ignored

    A. 3/4
    B. 1.5
    C. 3
    D. 4.5

Timed Exam 3 - 17. Draftstopping shall divide the concealed space into _____.

    A. manageable flame spread areas
    B. separate fire resistant domains
    C. ventilation segments
    D. approximately equal areas

Timed Exam 3 - 18. Which of the following locations is not always considered specific hazardous locations for the purposes of glazing.

     A. Glazing in storm doors
     B. Glazing in swinging doors except jalousies
     C. Glazing in fixed and sliding panels of sliding door assemblies and panels in sliding and bifold closet door assemblies
     D. Decorative glazing.
     E. All of the above

Timed Exam 3 - 19. Work shall not be done beyond the point indicated in each successive inspection without first obtaining _____.

     A. a permit for that section
     B. contractors approval
     C. the approval of the building official
     D. none of the above

Timed Exam 3 - 20. In dwellings or dwelling units with split levels and without an intervening door between the adjacent levels, a smoke alarm installed on the upper level shall suffice for the adjacent lower level provided that the lower level is less than _____.

     A. 4 feet below the upper level
     B. 8 feet below the upper level
     C. one full story below the upper level
     D. any of the above

Timed Exam 3 - 21. No building or structure shall be used or occupied, and no change in the existing occupancy classification of a building or structure or portion thereof shall be made until the building official has issued a _____.

     A. notice of compliance
     B. use permit
     C. certificate of occupancy
     D. none of the above

Timed Exam 3 - 22. Carports not open on _____ side(s) shall be considered a garage and shall comply with the provisions of this section for garages.

    A. one
    B. two
    C. three
    D. all four

Timed Exam 3 - 23. What is the minimum thickness of lumber floor sheathing in inches, where the floor joists are spaced 16 inches OC and is installed perpendicular to the joist.

    A. 11/16
    B. 5/8
    C. 3/4
    D. 1/2

Timed Exam 3 - 24. Does a 200 square foot garage floor have to have a vapor retarder under the concrete slab?

    A. Yes
    B. No
    C. Only if it is not heated.
    D. Only if it is heated.

Timed Exam 3 - 25. Foam plastic may be used in a roof covering assembly without a thermal barrier when the foam is separated from the interior of the building by wood structural panel sheathing not less than _____ inch in thickness bonded with exterior glue and identified as Exposure 1, with edge supported by blocking or tongue-and-groove joints.

    A. 15/32
    B. 1
    C. 1-15/32
    D. 1-3/4

Timed Exam 3 - 26. In dwelling units, where the opening of an operable window is located more than 72 inches above the finished grade or surface below, the lowest part of the clear opening of the window shall be a minimum of _____ inches above the finished floor of the room in which the window is located.

A. 4
B. 6
C. 8
D. 12

Timed Exam 3 - 27. Where eave or cornice vents are installed, insulation shall not block the free flow of air so that a minimum of a _____ inch(es) space shall be provided between the insulation and the roof sheathing at the location of the vent.

A. 1
B. 2
C. 3
D. 4

Timed Exam 3 - 28. The minimum net required ventilation for a crawl space under any building shall be provided with ventilation openings through foundation walls or exterior walls which are at least 1 square foot of area for each _____ square feet of under-floor space area, unless the ground surface is covered by a Class 1 vapor retarder material.

A. 150
B. 100
C. 75
D. 50

Timed Exam 3 - 29. Dwelling units in two-family dwellings shall be separated from each other by wall and/or floor assemblies having not less than _____ hour fire-resistance rating if equipped throughout with an automatic sprinkler system installed in accordance with NFPA 13.

A. 0
B. 1/2
C. 1
D. 2

142

½

60

m.d.a

Timed Exam 3 - 30. The minimum width for concrete and masonry footings for a 3 story conventional light frame construction dwelling where the soil load bearing value is 5000 psf is _____ inches.

A. 12
B. 15
C. 17
D. 29

Timed Exam 3 - 31. Handrails for stairways shall be continuous for the full length of the flight, from a point directly above the top riser of the flight to a point directly _____ lowest riser of the flight. Exceptions ignored.

A. above
B. perpendicular to the
C. parallel
D. none of the above

Timed Exam 3 - 32. A minimum 3-foot-by-3-foot landing shall be provided for a ramp _____.

A. At the top and bottom of ramps
B. Where doors open onto ramps
C. Where ramps change direction.
D. All of the above
E. None of the above

Timed Exam 3 - 33. The minimum headroom over a stairway shall not be less than _____ measured vertically from the sloped plane adjoining the tread nosing or from the floor surface of the landing or platform.

A. 6 feet 4 inches
B. 6 feet 8 inches
C. 6 feet 10 inches
D. 7 feet

Timed Exam 3 - 34. Flanges and lips of load-bearing cold-formed steel roof framing members _____.

    A. may be notched but not cut
    B. may be cut but not notched
    C. may be cut or notched
    D. shall not be cut or notched

Timed Exam 3 - 35. Utility grade studs shall not be spaced more than _____ inches on center, shall not support more than a roof and ceiling, and shall not exceed 8 feet in height for exterior walls and load-bearing walls or 10 feet for interior nonload-bearing walls.

    A. 16
    B. 19.2
    C. 24
    D. 32

Timed Exam 3 - 36. Backfill shall not be placed against the wall until the wall has sufficient strength and has been anchored to the floor above, or has been sufficiently _____ to prevent damage by the backfill.

    A. anchored
    B. examined
    C. braced
    D. none of the above

Timed Exam 3 - 37. The maximum riser height shall be _____ inches.

    A. 7.25
    B. 7.5
    C. 7.75
    D. 8

Timed Exam 3 - 38. Fences less than _____ feet high do not require a permit.

  A. 4
  B. 7
  C. 8
  D. 10

Timed Exam 3 - 39. A wood structural panel for a roof has a span rating of 32/16 it is 1/2 inch thick. What is the maximum span in inches for this panel if the edges are supported.

  A. 20
  B. 24
  C. 28
  D. 32

Timed Exam 3 - 40. What is the presumed load bearing value in pounds per square foot of silty sand,.

  A. 2,000
  B. 3,000
  C. 4,000
  D. 12,000

Timed Exam 3 - 41. Basements and every sleeping room shall have at least

_____ .

  A. one openable emergency escape and rescue opening
  B. two openable emergency escape and rescue openings
  C. one emergency escape and rescue opening
  D. two openable emergency escape and rescue opening

Timed Exam 3 - 42. Loose-fill insulation materials that cannot be mounted in the ASTM E 84 apparatus without a screen or artificial supports shall have a flame-spread rating not to exceed _____ with an accompanying smoke-developed factor not to exceed . Exceptions ignored.

  A. 50, 500
  B. 25, 450
  C. 75, 400
  D. none of the above

Timed Exam 3 - 43. All plumbing fixtures shall be connected to a sanitary sewer or to an _____.

    A. approved private sewage disposal system
    B. holding tank
    C. gravity flow pipe system to the outdoors
    D. any of the above

Timed Exam 3 - 44. Single station carbon monoxide alarms shall be listed as complying with _____ and shall be installed in accordance with this code and the manufacturer's installation instructions.

    A. UL 2034
    B. CE 4582
    C. NFPA Alarm code
    D. Any of these

3/4
90 min
2
0

Timed Exam 3 - 45. The minimum flange width in inches of cold formed steel joist with a web depth of 10 inches is _____.

    A. 2
    B. 1.75
    C. 1.5
    D. 1.625

Timed Exam 3 - 46. What are the required steel reinforcement rods for an 12 inch thick masonry foundation wall with a height of 9 feet with a unbalanced backfill height of 8 feet constructed in SC soil.

    A. #6 at 48" o.c.
    B. #4 at 48" o.c.
    C. #5 at 48" o.c.
    D. #6 at 56" o.c.

Timed Exam 3 - 47. Air exhaust and intake openings that terminate outdoors shall be protected with corrosion resistant screens, louvers or grilles having a minimum opening size of _____ inch and a maximum opening size of _____ inch in any dimension.

    A. 1/8, 1/4
    B. 1/2, 1
    C. 1/4, 1/2
    D. 3/8, 3/4

Timed Exam 3 - 48. Footings shall not bear on frozen soil unless _____.

    A. they reinforced with a minimum of two #4 rebars placed 4" from the bottom of the footing.
    B. it is sandy gravel soil type
    C. footings are a minimum of 30 inches wide and 8 inches deep
    D. such frozen condition is of a permanent character

Timed Exam 3 - 49. Openings which provide access to all under-floor spaces through a perimeter wall shall be not less than _____ inches .

    A. 16 X 24
    B. 16 X 22
    C. 18 X 24
    D. 18 X 30

Timed Exam 3 - 50. The building official is authorized to engage _____ as deemed necessary to report upon unusual technical issues that arise, subject to the approval of the appointing authority.

    A. an expert opinion
    B. in exploration
    C. scientific experiments
    D. none of the above

Timed Exam 3 - 51. Hearth extensions shall extend at least _____ inches front of and at least _____ inches beyond each side of the fireplace opening, where the fireplace opening is 6 square feet or less.

     A. 12, 12
     B. 20, 10
     C. 24, 6
     D. 16, 8

Timed Exam 3 - 52. What is design temperature that should be used in calculating insulation values for central Illinois, in degrees Ferinheight.

     A. -10
     B. 0
     C. +10
     D. +20

Timed Exam 3 - 53. An enclosed attic has a square footage of 2833 sf. What is the minimum free ventilation area required to vent this space. Exceptions ignored

     A. 6.3 sf
     B. 9.6 sf
     C. 18.9 sf
     D. 27.3 sf

Timed Exam 3 - 54. The building official shall issue all necessary _____ to ensure compliance with this code.

     A. permits
     B. certificates
     C. restrictions
     D. notices or orders

Timed Exam 3 - 55. A nosing not less than _____ inch(es) but not more than _____ inch(es) shall be provided on stairways with solid risers.

A. 1/2, 1-1/8
B. 1, 1-1/2
C. 5/8, 1-1/8
D. 3/4, 1-1/4

Timed Exam 3 - 56. Emergency escape and rescue openings shall have a minimum net clear opening of _____ on grade floor openings.

A. 7.5
B. 5.7
C. 5
D. 9

Timed Exam 3 - 57. All wood in contact with the ground, embedded in concrete in direct contact with the ground or embedded in concrete exposed to the weather that supports permanent structures intended for human occupancy shall be _____.
Exceptions ignored,

A. approved pressure preservative treated wood suitable for ground contact use
B. approved cedar or redwood
C. coated with 2 coats of black tar, creosote or formaldehyde.
D. any of the above

Timed Exam 3 - 58. Beams, girders or other concentrated loads supported by a wall or column shall have a bearing of at least 3 inches in length measured parallel to the beam upon solid masonry not less than _____ inches in thickness, or upon a metal bearing plate of adequate design and dimensions to distribute the load safely, or upon a continuous reinforced masonry member projecting not less than 4 inches from the face of the wall.

A. 1.5
B. 2
C. 3
D. 4

Timed Exam 3 - 59. When the header joist span does not exceed _____ feet, the header joist may be a single member the same size as the floor joist.

    A. 3
    B. 4
    C. 5
    D. 6

Timed Exam 3 - 60. When the building official issues a permit, the construction documents shall be approved in writing or by a stamp which states _____.

    A. REJECTED
    B. APPROVED
    C. OK
    D. REVIEWED FOR CODE COMPLIANCE

Timed Exam 4   2 Hours to Complete

Timed Exam 4 - 1.   All egress doors shall be readily openable from the side from which egress is to be made without the use of a

_____.

    A. door knob
    B. panic hardware bar
    C. key or special knowledge or effort
    D. any of the above

Timed Exam 4 - 2.   What is the maximum allowable span for #3 Hem-fir 2X10 floor joist space 16 inches OC with a live load of 30 psf and a dead load of 20 psf, in residential sleeping areas.

    A. 10feet 8 inches
    B. 10feet 2 inches
    C. 12feet 6 inches
    D. 11feet 8 inches

Timed Exam 4 - 3.   A comparative measure, expressed as a dimensionless number, derived from visual measurements of the spread of flame versus time for a material tested in accordance with ASTM E 84 or UL 723.

    A. FLAMABILITY INDEX
    B. FLAMABILITY TIME CONSTANT
    C. FLAME SPREAD INDEX
    D. NONE OF THESE

Timed Exam 4 - 4.   What is the minimum thickness of lumber floor sheathing in inches, where the floor joists are spaced 54 inches OC and is installed perpendicular to the joist.

    A. 11/16 T&G
    B. 3/4 T&G
    C. 5/8 T&G
    D. 1-1/2 T&G

Timed Exam 4 - 5.   Additions, alterations or repairs shall not cause a(n) _____ to become unsafe or adversely affect the performance of the building.

A. existing structure
B. new structure
C. temporary
D. none of the above

Timed Exam 4 - 6.   Masonry chimney walls shall be constructed of solid masonry units or hollow masonry units grouted solid with not less than a ____ inch nominal thickness.

A. 2
B. 3
C. 4
D. 6

Timed Exam 4 - 7.   Spiral stairways are permitted, provided the minimum width shall be _____ inches with each tread having a 71/2-inches minimum tread depth at 12 inches from the narrower edge.

A. 26
B. 30
C. 32
D. 36

Timed Exam 4 - 8.   What is the maximum allowable span for SS Douglas fir-larch 2X6 floor joist space 12 inches OC with a live load of 30 psf and a dead load of 10 psf, in residential sleeping areas.

A. 10feet 8 inches
B. 10feet 10 inches
C. 12feet 6 inches
D. 12feet 10 inches

Timed Exam 4 - 9. The construction of buildings and structures in accordance with the provisions of this code shall result in a system that provides a complete load path that meets all requirements for the transfer of all loads from their point of origin through the load resisting elements to the _____.

    A. floor
    B. exterior walls
    C. building structure
    D. foundation

Timed Exam 4 - 10. Glazing in walls, enclosures or fences containing or facing hot tubs, spas, whirlpools, saunas, steam rooms, bathtubs, showers and indoor or outdoor swimming pools where the bottom exposed edge of the glazing is less than ____ inches (1524 mm) measured vertically above any standing or walking surface shall be considered a hazardous location. This shall apply to single glazing and all panes in multiple glazing. Exceptions ignored.

    A. 96
    B. 72
    C. 60
    D. 48

Timed Exam 4 - 11. What is the maximum allowable span for cold-formed steel joists size 800S162-43 loaded with a live load of 40 PSF and spaced 16 inches OC.

    A. 15'-6"
    B. 15'-6"
    C. 12'-3"
    D. 14'-1"

Timed Exam 4 - 12. The grade away from foundation walls shall fall a minimum of_____ inches within the first _____ feet. Exceptions ignored.

    A. 10, 6
    B. 8, 12
    C. 12, 12
    D. 6, 10

Timed Exam 4 - 13. A permit shall not be valid until the
_____.

    A. fees have been paid
    B. plans are stamped
    C. construction has commenced
    D. day after issue

Timed Exam 4 - 14. An alternative material, design or method of construction shall be approved where the building official finds that the proposed design is satisfactory and complies with the intent of the provisions of this code, and that the material, method or work offered is, for the purpose intended,
_____.

    A. at least the equivalent of that prescribed in this code
    B. superior to that prescribed in this code
    C. even if it is not at least the equivalent of that prescribed in this code
    D. none of the above

Timed Exam 4 - 15. The _____ shall include excavations for thickened slabs intended for the support of bearing walls, partitions, structural supports, or equipment and special requirements for wood foundations.

    A. floodplain inspections
    B. frame and masonry inspection
    C. foundation inspection
    D. none of the above

Timed Exam 4 - 16. Handrail ends shall be returned or shall terminate in newel posts or _____.

    A. safety terminals
    B. above the risers
    C. at any point above the stairs
    D. none of the above

Timed Exam 4 - 17. The doubled cantilever back-span joists in cold-formed steel framed floors shall extend a minimum of _____ feet within the building.

A. 2
B. 4
C. 6
D. 8

Timed Exam 4 - 18. Wood columns shall not be less in nominal size than _____ and steel columns shall not be less than 3-inch-diameter standard pipe or approved equivalent.

A. 4 inches by 4 inches
B. 3 inches by 3 inches
C. 6 inches by 6 inches
D. none of the above

Timed Exam 4 - 19. Risers shall be vertical or sloped from the underside of the leading edge of the tread above at an angle not more than _____ degrees from the vertical.

A. 15
B. 30
C. 45
D. 60

Timed Exam 4 - 20. Braced wall lines with a length of _____ or less shall have a minimum of two braced wall panels of any length or one braced wall panel equal to _____ or more. Braced wall lines greater than _____ shall have a minimum of two braced wall panels.

A. 16 feet (4877 mm) , 48 inches (1219 mm), 16 feet (4877 mm)
B. 16 feet (4877 mm) , 16 feet (4877 mm), 16 feet (4877 mm)
C. 16 feet (4877 mm) , 48 inches (1219 mm), 48 inches (1219 mm)
D. 48 inches (1219 mm) , 48 inches (1219 mm), 16 feet (4877 mm)

Timed Exam 4 - 21. What are the required steel reinforcement rods for an 12 inch thick masonry foundation wall with a height of 8 feet with a unbalanced backfill height of 6 feet constructed in GM soil.

  A. #5 at 56" o.c.
  B. #4 at 72" o.c.
  C. #6 at 72" o.c.
  D. #4 at 56" o.c.

Timed Exam 4 - 22. Each dwelling unit shall be provided with a kitchen area and every kitchen area shall be provided with a _____.

  A. refrigerator
  B. sink
  C. countertop
  D. all of the above

Timed Exam 4 - 23. The requirements of this code are based on platform and _____ construction for light frame buildings.

  A. balloon frame
  B. wood frame
  C. steel frame
  D. all of the above

Timed Exam 4 - 24. Where joists, trusses or rafters are spaced more than 16 inches on center and the bearing studs below are spaced 24 inches on center, such members shall bear within _____ inches of the studs beneath.

  A. 8
  B. 6
  C. 5
  D. 2

Timed Exam 4 - 25. What is minimum specified compressive strength of concrete basement walls in psi, foundations and other concrete not exposed to the weather with moderate weathering potential.

A. 2500
B. 3000
C. 3500
D. 3750

Timed Exam 4 - 26. What is the maximum span for a girder constructed of 4 2X8s douglas fir-larch a building 36 feet wide and supporting the roof, ceiling and one center-bearing floor. The ground snow load in the area is 30 psf.

A. 4 feet 8 inches
B. 5 feet 8 inches
C. 5 feet 6 inches
D. 6 feet 7 inches

Timed Exam 4 - 27. What is the maximum stud spacing of 2X6 bearing walls when supporting two floors, roof and ceiling (inches).

A. 16
B. 19.2
C. 24
D. 32

Timed Exam 4 - 28. The diameter of holes bored or cut into members shall not exceed _____ the depth of the member.

A. 1/4
B. 1/3
C. 1/2
D. 2/3

Timed Exam 4 - 29. Ceilings in basements without habitable spaces may project to within _____ of the finished floor; and beams, girders, ducts or other obstructions may project to within _____ of the finished floor.

A. 6 feet, 10 inches, 6 feet, 4 inches
B. 6 feet, 10 inches, 6 feet, 8 inches
C. 6 feet, 4 inches, 6 feet, 4 inches
D. 6 feet, 8 inches, 6 feet, 4 inches

Timed Exam 4 - 30. The radius of curvature at the leading edge of a tread shall be no greater than _____ inch.

   A. 9/16
   B. 1/2
   C. 3/4
   D. 1 1/4

Timed Exam 4 - 31. When the code refers to LIB bracing as a braced wall line method, what does LIB stand for?

   A. Wind shear panel
   B. Wood shear plywood
   C. Wind structural-resistive panel
   D. Wood structural panel

Timed Exam 4 - 32. The width of a landing can not be less than the door served and every landing shall have a minimum dimension of _____ inches measured in the direction of travel.

   A. 36
   B. 40
   C. 44
   D. 48

Timed Exam 4 - 33. A stairway riser shall be measured vertically between leading edges of the adjacent treads with the greatest riser height within any flight of stairs not to exceed the smallest by more than _____ inch.

   A. .167
   B. .25
   C. .375
   D. .417

Timed Exam 4 - 34. In buildings with combustible ceiling or roof construction, an attic access opening shall be provided to attic areas that exceed _____ square feet and have a vertical height of _____ inches or greater.

    A. 30, 30
    B. 22, 30
    C. 18, 22
    D. 30, 22

Timed Exam 4 - 35. Every dwelling unit shall be provided with a water closet, lavatory, and a _____.

    A. bathtub
    B. shower
    C. bathtub or shower
    D. bathtub and shower

Timed Exam 4 - 36. Footings on or adjacent to slope surfaces shall be founded in material with an embedment and setback from the slope surface sufficient to provide vertical and lateral support for the footing without detrimental settlement if the slope is steeper than one unit vertical in one unit horizontal, the required setback shall be measured from an imaginary plane _____ degrees to the horizontal, projected upward from the toe of the slope.

    A. 15
    B. 30
    C. 45
    D. 60

Timed Exam 4 - 37. Handrails with a perimeter greater than _____ inches shall provide a graspable finger recess area on both sides of the profile.

    A. 4
    B. 5.5
    C. 6
    D. 61/4

Timed Exam 4 - 38. Handrail height, measured vertically from the sloped plane adjoining the tread nosing, or finish surface of ramp slope, shall be not less than _____ inches and not more than _____ inches. Exceptions ignored.

    A. 30, 40
    B. 32, 36
    C. 36, 40
    D. 34, 38

Timed Exam 4 - 39. The minimum thickness of galvanized steel valley lining material is _____ inches nominal.

    A. 0.0279
    B. 0.0379
    C. 0.0479
    D. 0.0179

Timed Exam 4 - 40. Reinforcement of web holes in cold steel formed floor joists not conforming to the requirements of the IRC shall be permitted if the hole is located fully within the center _____ percent of the span and the depth and length of the hole does not exceed _____ percent of the flat width of the web.

    A. 25, 65
    B. 30, 50
    C. 40, 50
    D. 40, 65
    E. none of the above

Timed Exam 4 - 41. It shall be the duty of the _____ to notify the building official that such work is ready for inspection.

    A. permit holder or their agent
    B. owner
    C. contractor
    D. none of the above

Timed Exam 4 - 42. Rafters shall be framed to ridge board or to each other with a gusset plate as a tie The ridge board shall be at least ____ inch(es) nominal thickness and not less in depth than the cut end of the rafter.

A. 1
B. 2
C. 1.5
D. 4

Timed Exam 4 - 43. No person shall make connections from a utility, source of energy, fuel or power to any building or system that is regulated by this code for which a permit is required,

_____.

     A. until approved by the utility
     B. until approved by the building official
     C. until the permit is issued
     D. none of the above

Timed Exam 4 - 44. The garage shall be separated from the residence and its attic area by not less than _____ applied to the garage side.

     A. 5/8-inch Type X gypsum board or equivalent
     B. 1/2-inch gypsum board or equivalent
     C. 3/4 inch fiberboard, plywood or 1/2 gypsum board
     D. non of the above

Timed Exam 4 - 45. In Townhouses, where roof surfaces adjacent to the wall or walls are at the same elevation, the parapet shall extend not less than _____ inches above the roof surfaces.

     A. 18
     B. 24
     C. 30
     D. 36

Timed Exam 4 - 46. A wood structural panel for a roof has a span rating of 24/16 it is 7/16 inch thick. What is the maximum span in inches for this panel if the edges are not supported.

     A. 12
     B. 16
     C. 24
     D. 28

Timed Exam 4 - 47. Open sides of stairs with a total rise of more than 30 inches above the floor or grade below shall have guards not less than _____ inches in height measured vertically from the nosing of the treads.

    A. 32
    B. 34
    C. 36
    D. 42

Timed Exam 4 - 48. What is the maximum allowable span for a 4 × 3 × 1/4 lintel supporting masonry veneer with one story above.

    A. 8'-0"
    B. 6'-0"
    C. 4'-6"
    D. 3'-0"

Timed Exam 4 - 49. The maximum slope for a ramp is one unit vertical in _____ units horizontal.

    A. twelve
    B. ten
    C. eight
    D. six

Timed Exam 4 - 50. On exterior walls that require bracing, walls parallel to a braced wall that are part of that bracing structure line shall be offset not more than _____ from the designated braced wall line location.

    A. 1 foot (304 mm)
    B. 2 feet (609 mm)
    C. 4 feet (1219 mm)
    D. 6 feet (1829 mm)

Timed Exam 4 - 51. Masonry chimneys shall be supported on foundations of solid masonry or concrete at least _____ inches thick and at least inches beyond each side of the exterior dimensions of the chimney.

    A. 12, 6
    B. 10, 5
    C. 16, 8
    D. 8, 6

Timed Exam 4 - 52. The minimum headroom above a spiral staircase is

_____.

    A. 6 feet 6 inches
    B. 6 feet 8 inches
    C. 6 feet 4 inches
    D. 7 feet

Timed Exam 4 - 53. Access shall be provided to all under-floor spaces with the minimum size of openings through the floor to be
_____ inches .

    A. 16 X 22
    B. 18 X 30
    C. 18 X 24
    D. 22 X 30

Timed Exam 4 - 54. Solid masonry walls of one-story dwellings and garages shall not be less than _____ inches in thickness when not greater than _____ feet in height, provided that when gable construction is used, an additional _____ feet is permitted to the peak of the gable.

    A. 9, 6, 6
    B. 9, 6, 9
    C. 8, 6, 6
    D. 6, 9, 6

Timed Exam 4 - 55. The purpose of the IRC is to establish
_____ requirements to safeguard the public safety, health and
general welfare through affordability, structural strength, means of egress
facilities, stability, sanitation, light and ventilation, energy conservation and
safety to life and property from fire and other hazards attributed to the built
environment and to provide safety to fire fighters and emergency responders
during emergency operations.

    A. standard
    B. maximum
    C. minimum
    D. limited

Timed Exam 4 - 56. Joists framing into the side of a wood girder shall be
supported by approved framing anchors or on ledger strips not less than
nominal _____.

    A. 2 X 2
    B. 2 X 4
    C. 1 X 4
    D. 2 X 6

Timed Exam 4 - 57. Where it is necessary to make an inspection to enforce the
provisions of this code, is authorized to enter the structure or premises at
_____ to inspect or to perform the duties imposed by this code,
provided that if such structure or premises be occupied that credentials be
presented to the occupant and entry requested.

    A. any time
    B. unannounced
    C. reasonable times
    D. all of the above

Timed Exam 4 - 58. The bracing required for each building shall be determined
by circumscribing a rectangle around the entire building on each floor. The
rectangle shall surround all enclosed offsets and projections such as sunrooms
and attached garages. Open structures, such as carports and decks, shall be
permitted to be excluded. The rectangle shall have no side greater than
_____, and the ratio between the long side and short side shall
be a maximum of _____.

A. 160 feet (18 288 mm), 3:1
B. 60 feet (18 288 mm), 3:1
C. 60 feet (18 288 mm), 4:1
D. 120 feet (18 288 mm), 6:1

Timed Exam 4 - 59. For a truss framed roof in wind exposure category B, with the trusses spaces 16" OC, and a roof span of 28 feet, if the basic wind design speed is 100 mph what is the uplift force on the each truss connection to the top plate of the wall? The roof pitch is 12:12,

A. 189
B. 251
C. 269
D. 217

Timed Exam 4 - 60. The illumination of exterior stairways shall be controlled from _____ the dwelling unit.

A. inside
B. outside

Timed Exam 5   2 Hours to Complete

Timed Exam 5 - 1.   What is the presumed load bearing value in pounds per square foot of silty clay.

    A. 1,500
    B. 2,500
    C. 3,500
    D. 4,000

Timed Exam 5 - 2.   What is the maximum span for a girder constructed of 3 2X10s douglas fir-larch a building 28 feet wide and supporting the roof, ceiling and two clear span floors. The ground snow load in the area is 30 psf.

    A. 5 feet 1 inches
    B. 6 feet 4 inches
    C. 5 feet 8 inches
    D. 7 feet 6 inches

Timed Exam 5 - 3.   The triangular openings formed by the riser, tread and bottom rail of a guard at the open side of a stairway are permitted to be of such a size that a sphere _____ inches cannot pass through.

    A. 4
    B. 6
    C. 8
    D. 12

Timed Exam 5 - 4.   Wood columns shall be approved
_____. Exceptions ignored.

    A. wood of natural decay resistance
    B. pressure preservatively treated wood
    C. either of the above
    D. none of the above

Timed Exam 5 - 5. Enclosed accessible space under stairs shall have walls, under stair surface and any soffits protected on the enclosed side with 1/ 2 inch _____.

    A. sheathing material
    B. gypsum board
    C. fiberboard or OSB
    D. any of the above

Timed Exam 5 - 6. Which of the following does not require a permit.

    A. Prefabricated swimming pools that are less than 36 inches deep.
    B. Swings and other playground equipment.
    C. Window awnings supported by an exterior wall which do not project more than 80 inches from the exterior wall and do not require additional support.
    D. all of the above

Timed Exam 5 - 7. All exposed insulation materials installed on attic floors shall have a critical radiant flux not less than _____ watt per square centimeter.

    A. 0.12
    B. 0.25
    C. 1.25
    D. 3.75

Timed Exam 5 - 8. The bottom surface of footings shall not have a slope exceeding one unit vertical in _____ units horizontal .

    A. 12
    B. 10
    C. 6
    D. 8

Timed Exam 5 - 9.   All spaces between chimneys and floors and ceilings through which chimneys pass shall be _____ with noncombustible material securely fastened in place.

    A. fireproofed
    B. smokeproofed
    C. fireblocked
    D. any of the above

Timed Exam 5 - 10. Notches in solid lumber joists, rafters and beams shall not exceed _____ of the depth of the member, shall not be longer than _____ of the depth of the member and shall not be located in the middle _____ of the span.

    A. one-sixth, one-third, one-half
    B. one-third, one-third, one-third
    C. one-sixth, one-third, one-third
    D. one-sixth, one-half, one-third

Timed Exam 5 - 11. Cold formed steel floor cantilevered joist shall be permitted only on the _____ of a two-story building or the first floor of a one-story building if the cantilevered joists are not doubled.

    A. first floor
    B. second floor

Timed Exam 5 - 12. Bathrooms, water closet compartments and other similar rooms shall be provided with aggregate glazing area in windows of not less than _____ square feet, one-half of which must be openable. Exceptions ignored.

    A. 3
    B. 6
    C. 9
    D. 12

Timed Exam 5 - 13. Spiral stairways shall have all treads identical, and the rise shall be no more than _____ inches.

  A. 7 3/4
  B. 8 1/2
  C. 9
  D. 9 1/2

Timed Exam 5 - 14. Owner-occupied lodging houses with _____ guestrooms shall be permitted to be constructed in accordance with the International Residential Code for One- and Two-family Dwellings when equipped with a fire sprinkler system.

  A. two or fewer
  B. three or fewer
  C. four or fewer
  D. five or fewer

Timed Exam 5 - 15. The minimum width of a hallway shall be not less than _____.

  A. 3 feet
  B. 38 inches
  C. 36 inches
  D. A and C

Timed Exam 5 - 16. Floor assemblies, not required elsewhere in this code to be fire-resistance rated, shall be provided with a _____ gypsum wallboard membrane, 5/8-inch (16 mm) wood structural panel membrane, or equivalent on the underside of the floor framing member. Exceptions ignored.

  A. 3/8-inch (9.5 mm)
  B. 1/2-inch (12.7 mm)
  C. 5/8-inch (15.9 mm)
  D. 3/4-inch (19.0 mm)

Timed Exam 5 - 17. What is the maximum rafter span for #1 Southern pine 2X8 spaced 16 inches OC with a ground snow load of 30 PSF and a dead load of 10 PSF with the ceiling not attached to the rafters.

    A. 14-7
    B. 14-7
    C. 18-1
    D. 19-9

Timed Exam 5 - 18. Bars, grills, covers, screens or similar devices are permitted to be placed over emergency escape and rescue openings, bulkhead enclosures, or windowwells that serve such openings, provided the minimum net clear opening size complies with the code and such devices shall be _____ from the inside without the use of a key, tool, special knowledge or force greater than that which is required for normal operation of the escape and rescue opening.

    A. releasable
    B. removable
    C. releasable or removable
    D. any of the above

Timed Exam 5 - 19. Ducts in the garage and ducts penetrating the walls or ceilings separating the dwelling from the garage shall be constructed of a minimum No. _____ gage sheet steel or other approved material and shall have no openings into the garage.

    A. 30
    B. 24
    C. 26
    D. 20

Timed Exam 5 - 20. Any wood stud in an exterior wall or bearing partition may be cut or notched to a depth not exceeding _____ percent of its width.

    A. 25
    B. 35
    C. 40
    D. 60

Timed Exam 5 - 21. Each townhouse shall be _____
and shall be separated by fire resistance rated wall assemblies meeting the
requirements of Section R302 for exterior walls. Exceptions ignored.

     A. considered a separate building
     B. considered part of the same building
     C. fire resistance dependent on the other unit.
     D. none of the above

Timed Exam 5 - 22. Joists shall be supported laterally at the ends by full-depth
solid blocking not less than _____ inches nominal in thickness; or by
attachment to a full depth header, band, or rim joist, or to an adjoining stud, or
shall be otherwise provided with lateral support to prevent rotation. Exceptions
ignored.

     A. 1
     B. 2
     C. 3
     D. 4

Timed Exam 5 - 23. Fire resistance rated floor ceiling and wall assemblies
shall extend to and be tight against the exterior wall, and wall assemblies shall
extend _____. Exceptions ignored.

     A. through the roof
     B. to the underside of the roof sheathing
     C. beyond the roof to a minimum height of 30 inches
     D. none of the above

Timed Exam 5 - 24. "The IRC Code regulates the construction of steel floor
framing for buildings not greater than _____ feet in length perpendicular to the
joist span, not greater than _____ feet in width parallel to the joist span, and
less than
or equal to _____ stories above grade plane"

     A. 60, 60, 2
     B. 60, 28,3
     C. 60, 40, 3
     D. 40, 36, 3

Timed Exam 5 - 25. The minimum thickness of masonry bearing walls more than one story high shall be _____ inches.

    A. 6
    B. 7
    C. 8
    D. 10

Timed Exam 5 - 26. Egress doors shall be readily openable from inside the dwelling without the use of a _____ or special knowledge or effort.

    A. key
    B. bolt
    C. latch
    D. deadbolt

Timed Exam 5 - 27. The use of a volute, turnout, starting easing or starting newel shall be allowed over the _____ tread.

    A. last
    B. first
    C. first and last
    D. lowest

Timed Exam 5 - 28. Buildings shall have approved address numbers, building numbers or approved building identification placed in a position that is plainly legible and visible from the street or road fronting the property. These numbers shall contrast with their background. Address numbers shall be Arabic numbers or alphabetical letters. Numbers shall be a minimum of _____ high with a minimum stroke width of _____. Where access is by means of a private road and the building address cannot be viewed from the public way, a monument, pole or other sign or means shall be used to identify the structure.

    A. 3 inches (77 mm), 1/2 inch (12.7 mm)
    B. 4 inches (102 mm), 1/2 inch (12.7 mm)
    C. 4 inches (102 mm), 1/4 inch (6.4 mm)
    D. 6 inches (153 mm), 1/2 inch (12.7 mm)

Timed Exam 5 - 29. The building official, member of the board of appeals or employee charged with the enforcement of this code, while acting for the jurisdiction in good faith and without malice in the discharge of the duties required by this code or other pertinent law or ordinance, _____ for any damage accruing to persons or property as a result of any act or by reason of an act or omission in the discharge of official duties.

      A. shall thereby be rendered liable personally and is hereby personally liability
      B. shall not thereby be rendered liable personally and is hereby personally liability
      C. shall thereby be rendered liable personally and is hereby relieved from personal liability
      D. shall not thereby be rendered liable personally and is hereby relieved from personal liability

Timed Exam 5 - 30. The top flanges of steel joists shall be laterally braced by the application of floor sheathing fastened to the joists. Floor joists with spans that exceed _____ feet shall have the bottom flanges laterally braced.

      A. 6
      B. 8
      C. 12
      D. 14

Timed Exam 5 - 31. Notches in flanges and lips of load-bearing steel floor framing members shall _____.

      A. be a maximum of 1/2 of the flange width
      B. be allowed if they are closer than 10 inches from bearing ends
      C. not be allowed
      D. none of these

Timed Exam 5 - 32. Flue lining systems for gas appliances shall be in accordance with Chapter _____.

      A. 20
      B. 23
      C. 24
      D. 27

Timed Exam 5 - 33. Single trimmer joists may be used to carry a single header joist that is located within _____ feet of the trimmer joist bearing.

      A. 3
      B. 4
      C. 5
      D. 6

Timed Exam 5 - 34. What is the minimum wall thickness in inches for a plain masonry foundation wall with a height of 6 feet with a unbalanced backfill height of 5 feet constructed in sandy gravel soil.

      A. 6 solid or 8
      B. 10 solid
      C. 12
      D. 10

Timed Exam 5 - 35. When the code refers to LIB bracing as a braced wall line method, what does LIB stand for?

      A. Lateral-inline-bracing
      B. Let-in-bracing
      C. Lumber-inline-bracing
      D. Lumber-internally-braced

Timed Exam 5 - 36. Open stair risers are permitted if the opening between treads does not permit the passage of a _____ inch diameter sphere.

      A. 4
      B. 6
      C. 7
      D. 8

Timed Exam 5 - 37. The provisions of the International Residential Code applies to the construction of detached one and two family dwellings and multiple single-family dwellings not more than _____ stories in height with a separate means of egress and their accessory structures.

    A. one
    B. two
    C. three
    D. four

Timed Exam 5 - 38. Steel fireplace units are permitted to be installed with solid masonry to form a masonry fireplace when installed either according to the requirements of their listing or according to the requirements of this section. Steel fireplace units incorporating a steel firebox lining, shall be constructed with steel not less than _____ inch in thickness, and an air circulating chamber which is ducted to the interior of the building.

    A. 1/8
    B. 1/4
    C. 3/8
    D. 1/16

Timed Exam 5 - 39. Bathrooms shall have a minimum ceiling height of _____ at the center of the front clearance area for fixtures.

    A. 7 feet — 6' 8"
    B. 6 feet 10 inches
    C. 6 feet 6 inches
    D. 7 feet 2 inches
                    P 54   R 305

Timed Exam 5 - 40. The ends of each joist, beam or girder shall have not less than _____ inches of bearing on masonry or concrete. Exceptions ignored

    A. 1.5
    B. 2
    C. 3
    D. 4

Timed Exam 5 - 41. Winder stair treads shall have a minimum tread depth of
_____ inches at any point.

A. 6
B. 8
C. 10
D. 12

Timed Exam 5 - 42. What is the minimum R value for insulation installed in a
exterior building wood frame wall in a single family dwelling in Marathon County
Wisconsin.

A. R-21
B. R-13
C. R-19
D. R20 or R13 + 5
E. C or D

Timed Exam 5 - 43. Columns shall be restrained to prevent lateral
displacement at the _____ end(s).

A. bottom
B. top
C. both
D. any of the above

Timed Exam 5 - 44. Where lot lines, walls, slopes or other physical barriers
prohibit _____ inches of fall within 10 feet for surface drainage, Impervious
surfaces within 10 feet (3048 mm) of the building foundation shall be sloped a
minimum of _____ percent away from the building

A. 4, 5
B. 6, 2
C. 8, 2
D. 10, 6

Timed Exam 5 - 45. Slump of concrete placed in removable forms shall not exceed _____. Exceptions ignored.

    A. 4 inches (101mm)
    B. 6 inches (152 mm)
    C. 8 inches (203 mm)
    D. 12 inches (304 mm)

Timed Exam 5 - 46. Insulation materials, including facings, such as vapor retarders or vapor permeable membranes installed within floor-ceiling assemblies, roof-ceiling assemblies, wall assemblies, crawl spaces and attics shall have a flame-spread index not to exceed _____ with an accompanying smoke-developed index not to exceed. Exceptions ignored.

    A. 25, 450
    B. 50, 600
    C. 65, 450
    D. 25, 200

Timed Exam 5 - 47. Handrails shall not project more than _____ inches on either side of the stairway.

    A. 2.5
    B. 3
    C. 4
    D. 4.5

Timed Exam 5 - 48. For roof slopes of four units vertical in 12 units horizontal or greater, underlayment shall be a minimum of one layer of underlayment felt applied shingle fashion, parallel to and starting from the eaves and lapped _____ inches, fastened sufficiently in place.

    A. 1
    B. 2
    C. 4
    D. 6

Timed Exam 5 - 49. The minimum width for concrete and masonry footings for a 2 story conventional light frame construction dwelling where the soil load bearing value is 3000 psf is _____ inches.

    A. 12
    B. 15
    C. 17
    D. 24

Timed Exam 5 - 50. Chimneys shall extend at least _____ feet higher than any portion of a building within _____ feet, but shall not be less than _____ feet above the highest point where the chimney passes through the roof.

    A. 3, 12, 6
    B. 4, 4, 3
    C. 2, 10, 3
    D. 2, 8, 3

Timed Exam 5 - 51. How many jack studs are required under each end of a header made from 2 2X10s hem-fir supporting one floor only on a 28 foot wide building.   The ground snow load is 50 psf.

    A. 1
    B. 2
    C. 3
    D. 4

Timed Exam 5 - 52. Carports shall be open on _____.

    A. at least one side
    B. at least two sides
    C. at least three sides
    D. all four sides

Timed Exam 5 - 53. Lateral ties in masonry columns shall be spaced not more than _____ inches on center and shall be at least 3/8 inch diameter. Lateral ties shall be embedded in grout.

A. 4
B. 6
C. 8   6069.2.2
D. 12

Timed Exam 5 - 54. What is the maximum cantilever span for 2X10 floor joists 24 inches oc, with a ground snow load of 50 psf.

    A. 20 inches
    B. 40 inches
    C. 48 inches
    D. 60 inches

Timed Exam 5 - 55. For a truss framed roof in wind exposure category B, with the trusses spaces 24" OC, and a roof span of 32 feet, if the basic wind design speed is 90 mph what is the uplift force on the each truss connection to the top plate of the wall? The roof pitch is 5:12,

    A. 50
    B. 200
    C. 150
    D. 175

Timed Exam 5 - 56. _____ shall be permitted to be backfilled prior to inspection.

    A. Underground plumbing pipes
    B. Under slab electrical conduits and raceways
    C. Under slab gas piping
    D. Ground-source heat pump loop systems tested in accordance with
Section M2105.1

Timed Exam 5 - 57. Which of the following is not listed as contained on a certificate of occupancy.

    A. The name of the contractor
    "B. Any special stipulations and conditions of the building
permit."
    C. The name of the building official.
    D. The building permit number.

Timed Exam 5 - 58. Where equipment replacements and repairs must be performed in an emergency situation, _____.

    A. the permit application shall be submitted before any work can begin
    B. no permit is needed
    C. the permit application shall be submitted within the next working business day
    D. none of the above

Timed Exam 5 - 59. Concrete and masonry foundation walls shall extend above the finished grade adjacent to the foundation at all points a minimum of _____ inches where masonry veneer is used and a minimum of _____ inches elsewhere.

    A. 6, 8
    B. 8, 10
    C. 4, 6
    D. 6, 4

Timed Exam 5 - 60. In Table R502.3.1(1) Floor Joist Spans For Common Lumber Species (Residential Sleeping Areas, Live Load = 30 Psf, what maximum deflection are the values in the table based on.

    A. $L/\Delta = 360$
    B. $L/\Delta = 240$
    C. $L/\Delta = 120$
    D. $L/\Delta = 180$

Timed Exam 6   2 Hours to Complete

Timed Exam 6 - 1. Glazing in railings with and area of _____ sq. ft. or a height of _____ inches above a walking surface are considered hazardous locations.

    A. 9, 36
    B. 12, 42
    C. 6, 30
    D. All glazing in railings regardless of an area or height

Timed Exam 6 - 2. Slate shingles shall only be used on slopes of _____ units vertical in 12 units horizontal or greater.

    A. 2
    B. 3
    C. 4
    D. 6

Timed Exam 6 - 3. What are the required steel reinforcement rods for an 9.5 inch thick concrete foundation wall with a height of 8 feet with a unbalanced backfill height of 7 feet constructed in GM soil.

    A. #4 at 24" o.c.
    B. #4 at 32" o.c.
    C. #6 at 32" o.c.
    D. Plain Concrete, none

Timed Exam 6 - 4. What is the presumed load bearing value in pounds per square foot of sandy gravel and/or gravel.

    A. 1,000
    B. 1,500
    C. 3,000
    D. 4,000

Timed Exam 6 - 5.   Wood-framed buildings shall be limited to _____ stories above grade plane or the limits given in Table R602.10.3(3).

    A. Two
    B. Three
    C. Four
    D. Five

Timed Exam 6 - 6.   What is the maximum ceiling joist span for SS Douglas fir-larch 2X8 spaced 19.2 inches OC with a live load of 20 PSF and a dead load of 10 PSF in an uninhabitable attics without storage.

    A. 17-1
    B. 18-5
    C. 24-0
    D. 15-2

Timed Exam 6 - 7.   Footings shall be _____ where it is necessary to change the elevation of the top surface of the footings or where the slope of the bottom surface of the footings will exceed one unit vertical in ten units horizontal.

    A. reinforced with rebar
    B. increased in depth
    C. leveled
    D. stepped

Timed Exam 6 - 8.   Foam plastics may be used without a thermal barrier when the foam plastic is protected by a minimum _____ inch(es) thickness of masonry or concrete.

    A. 1
    B. 2
    C. 3
    D. 4

Timed Exam 6 - 9.   The maximum smoke-developed index of wall and ceiling finishes shall not exceed _____.

    A. 300
    B. 700
    C. 450
    D. 900

Timed Exam 6 - 10. In the case of demolition, the site plan shall show construction to be _____ and the location and size of existing structures and construction that are to remain on the site or plot. The building official is authorized to waive or modify the requirement for a site plan when the application for permit is for alteration or repair or when otherwise warranted.

    A. erected
    B. moved
    C. demolished
    D. none of these

Timed Exam 6 - 11. Exhaust air shall not be directed onto _____.

    A. walkways
    B. the road
    C. beyond the minimum CFM
    D. a roof

Timed Exam 6 - 12. The walking surface of treads and landings of stairways shall be sloped no steeper than _____.

    A. 1-percent slope
    B. 2-percent slope
    C. 3-percent slope
    D. 4-percent slope

Timed Exam 6 - 13. Garages beneath habitable rooms shall be separated from all habitable rooms above by not less than

_____ or equivalent.

 A. 1/2 inch gypsum board
 B. 5/8 inch gypsum board
 C. 1/2 inch Type X gypsum board
 D. 5/8 inch Type X gypsum board

Timed Exam 6 - 14. Subflooring may be omitted when joist spacing does not exceed _____ inches and a 1-inch nominal tongue-and-groove wood strip flooring is applied perpendicular to the joists.

 A. 12
 B. 16
 C. 19.2
 D. 24

Timed Exam 6 - 15. A (An) _____ residential fire sprinkler system shall be installed in one- and two- family dwellings.

 A. Copper or brass
 B. automatic
 C. remote control
 D. none of these

Timed Exam 6 - 16. A wood structural panel for a subfloor has a span rating of 24/16 it is 7/16 inch thick. What is the allowable live load in psf for this panel if the floor joists are spaced 16" o.c.

 A. 30
 B. 50
 C. 100
 D. 180

Timed Exam 6 - 17. This describes type SP soil type.

    A. Well-graded gravels, gravel sand mixtures, little or no fines.
    B. Poorly graded gravels or gravel sand mixtures, little or no fines.
    C. Well-graded sands, gravelly sands, little or no fines.
    D. Poorly graded sands or gravelly sands, little or no fines.

Timed Exam 6 - 18. What is the minimum wall thickness in inches for a plain masonry foundation wall with a height of 8 feet with a unbalanced backfill height of 7 feet constructed in sandy gravel soil.

    A. 6
    B. 8
    C. 10
    D. 12

Timed Exam 6 - 19. The greatest stair nosing projection shall not exceed the smallest nosing projection by more than _____ inch between two stories, including the nosing at the level of floors and landings.

    A. 1/4
    B. 3/8
    C. 1/2
    D. 3/4

Timed Exam 6 - 20. Bathtub and shower floors and walls above bath tubs with installed shower heads and in shower compartments shall be finished with

_____

    A. ceramic tile
    B. glass, tile, marble or other hard material
    C. a nonabsorbent surface
    D. a watertight enclosure

Timed Exam 6 - 21. There shall be a floor or landing at the _____ of each stairway. Exceptions ignored.

    A. top
    B. bottom
    C. top and bottom
    D. all of the above

Timed Exam 6 - 22. All unit skylights installed in a roof with a pitch flatter than _____ units vertical in 12 units horizontal shall be mounted on a curb extending at least _____ inches above the plane of the roof unless otherwise specified in the manufacturer's installation instructions.

    A. two, 6
    B. three, 6
    C. four, 6
    D. three, 4

Timed Exam 6 - 23. Fireblocking of cornices of a two-family dwelling is required at _____.

    A. between basement areas
    B. between garage areas
    C. 8 foot intervals
    D. at the line of dwelling unit separation

Timed Exam 6 - 24. Bathtub and shower floors and walls above bathtubs with installed shower heads and in shower compartments shall be finished with a nonabsorbent surface that extend to a height of not less than _____ above the floor.

    A. 6 feet
    B. 7 feet
    C. 6 feet 8 inches
    D. 6 feet 10 inches

Timed Exam 6 - 25. When alterations, repairs or additions requiring a permit occur, or when one or more sleeping rooms are added or created in existing dwellings, the individual dwelling unit shall be equipped with smoke alarms located as required for new dwellings unless the permit is for work

_____,

A. involving the exterior surfaces of dwellings, such as the replacement of roofing or siding.
B. the addition or replacement of windows or doors.
C. the addition of a porch or deck as in the 2009 INTERNATIONAL RESIDENTIAL CODE® BUILDING PLANNING.
D. any of the above

Timed Exam 6 - 26. Additions, alterations or repairs to any structure shall conform to that required for a new structure _____ the existing structure to comply with all of the requirements of this code, unless otherwise stated.

A. shall require
B. must require
C. without requiring
D. none of the above

Timed Exam 6 - 27. In geographical areas where experience has shows a specific need, approved naturally durable or pressure-preservative-treated wood may be used for those portions of the wood structure or other parts that form the structural supports of buildings, balconies, porches or similar permanent building part when those members are exposed to the elements without enough protection from a roof, eave, overhang or other covering that would inhibit moisture or water gathering on the surface or at joints between members. If Local experience dictates, these members can include:

A. Horizontal members such as girders, joists and decking.
B. Vertical members such as posts, poles and columns. 3.
C. Both horizontal and vertical members.
D. any or all of the above.

Timed Exam 6 - 28. What is the maximum allowable length (in feet) of wood wall studs exposed to wind speeds of 100 mph or less in seismic design categories a, b, c and d, for 2X6 studs supporting one floor and a roof 16 inches OC.

    A. 10
    B. 12
    C. 16
    D. 18

Timed Exam 6 - 29. Smoke alarms shall receive their primary power from _____. Exceptions ignored.

    A. a emergency power source
    B. a battery UPS system
    C. the building wiring
    D. the battery within each unit

Timed Exam 6 - 30. When supported by steel-framed walls, cold-formed steel floor framing shall be constructed with floor joists located directly in-line with load-bearing studs located below the joists with a maximum tolerance of _____ inch between the center lines of the joist and the stud.

    A. 1/2
    B. 3/4
    C. 1
    D. 3/8

Timed Exam 6 - 31. Every dwelling unit shall have at least one habitable room that shall have not less than _____ square feet of gross floor area.

    A. 90
    B. 100
    C. 120
    D. 180

Timed Exam 6 - 32. Tail joists over _____ feet long shall be supported at the header by framing anchors or on ledger strips not less than 2 inches by 2 inches.

    A. 8
    B. 10
    C. 12
    D. 14

Timed Exam 6 - 33. Glazing in an individual fixed or operable panel adjacent to a door where the nearest vertical edge of the glazing is within a _____ inch arc of either vertical edge of the door in a closed position and where the bottom exposed edge of the glazing is less than _____ inches above the floor or walking surface shall be considered a hazardous location.

    A. 24, 60
    B. 78, 78
    C. 72, 72
    D. 48, 48

Timed Exam 6 - 34. Wood framing supporting gypsum board shall not be less than ____ inches nominal thickness in the least dimension except that wood furring strips not less than 1X2 inch nominal dimension may be used over solid backing or framing spaced not more than ____ inches on center.

    A. 2, 24
    B. 4, 16
    C. 3, 16
    D. 1.5, 16

Timed Exam 6 - 35. Freestanding accessory structures with an area of _____ square feet or less and an eave height of 10 feet or less shall not be required to be protected from frost.

    A. 100
    B. 200
    C. 300
    D. 400

Timed Exam 6 - 36. The landing at an exterior doorway shall not be more than _____ inches below the top of the threshold, provided the door, other than an exterior storm or screen door does not swing over the landing.

    A. .25
    B. .75
    C. 1.5
    D. 7.75

Timed Exam 6 - 37. The smoke-developed rating shall _____ where foam plastic is used in a roof covering assembly without a thermal barrier when the foam is separated from the interior of the building by wood structural panel sheathing not less than 15/32 inch in thickness bonded with exterior glue and identified as Exposure 1, with edge supported by blocking or tongue-and-groove joints

    A. be not more than 450
    B. be not less than 450
    C. be not more than 600
    D. not be limited

Timed Exam 6 - 38. The minimum openable area to the outdoors shall be _____ percent of the floor area being ventilated.

    A. 4
    B. 6
    C. 8
    D. 10

Timed Exam 6 - 39. Ends of ceiling joists shall be lapped a minimum of _____ inches or butted over bearing partitions or beams and toenailed to the bearing member.

    A. 2
    B. 3
    C. 4
    D. 6

Timed Exam 6 - 40. Truss members and components shall not be cut, notched, spliced or otherwise altered in anyway without the approval of _____.

    A. the IRC
    B. a professional contractor
    C. a residential designer
    D. a registered design professional.

Timed Exam 6 - 41. Wood basement floors shall be limited to applications where the differential depth of fill on opposite exterior foundation walls is _____ feet or less, unless special provision is made to resist sliding caused by unbalanced lateral soil loads.

    A. 2
    B. 4
    C. 5
    D. 6

Timed Exam 6 - 42. What is the minimum thickness of lumber floor sheathing in inches, where the floor joists are spaced 24 inches OC and is installed perpendicular to the joist.

    A. 11/16
    B. 5/8
    C. 3/4
    D. 1

Timed Exam 6 - 43. Exterior landings, decks, balconies, stairs and similar facilities shall be positively anchored to the primary structure to resist both vertical and lateral forces or shall be designed to be self-supporting. Attachment shall not be accomplished by use of _____.

    A. joist hangers
    B. cantilevers
    C. lag bolts
    D. toenails

Timed Exam 6 - 44. Where basements contain one or more sleeping rooms, emergency egress and rescue openings shall be required in each sleeping room, _____.

    A. but shall not be required in adjoining areas of the basement
    B. and shall also be required in adjoining areas of the basement
    C. unless there are emergency egress and rescue openings in adjoining areas of the basement
    D. none of the above

Timed Exam 6 - 45. Doors between the garage and residence shall be equipped with solid wood doors not less than _____ inches in thickness, solid or honeycomb core steel doors not less than _____ inches thick, or _____ minute fire rated doors.

    A. 13/8, 13/8, 30
    B. 13/8, 13/8, 20
    C. 13/4, 13/4, 20
    D. 13/8, 13/8, 60

Timed Exam 6 - 46. The minimum stairway tread depth shall be _____ inches.

    A. 9.25
    B. 10
    C. 10.5
    D. 11

Timed Exam 6 - 47. A floor or landing is not required at the top of an interior flight of stairs, provided a door _____.

    A. has a safety catch type latch
    B. has a window allowing the occupant to see the stairway on the other side
    C. has a sign indicating that there is a stairway on the other side.
    D. does not swing over the stairs

Timed Exam 6 - 48. Wood studs in nonbearing partitions may be notched to a depth not to exceed _____ percent of a single stud width.

    A. 60
    B. 35
    C. 25
    D. 40

Timed Exam 6 - 49. _____ is required at all interconnections between concealed vertical and horizontal spaces such as occur at soffits, drop ceilings and cove ceilings.

    A. Draftstopping
    B. Smoke barriers
    C. Fireblocking
    D. non of the above

Timed Exam 6 - 50. Where, in any specific case, different sections of this code specify different materials, methods of construction or other requirements, the _____ shall govern.

    A. least restrictive
    B. most restrictive
    C. most economical
    D. environmentally friendly

Timed Exam 6 - 51. Structural capacities and design provisions for prefabricated wood I-joists shall be established and monitored in accordance with _____.

    A. ASTM E 2214
    B. APA 13A
    C. ASTM D 5055
    D. APWI 1525

Timed Exam 6 - 52. Handrails on a ramp adjacent to a wall shall have a space of not less than _____inches between the wall and the handrails.

    A. 2
    B. 2.5
    C. 1.75
    D. 1.5

Timed Exam 6 - 53. What is the cross-sectional area of a round flue 8 inches in diameter (answer is in square inches)

    A. 28
    B. 38
    C. 50
    D. 64

Timed Exam 6 - 54. What is the maximum spacing for framing members for a ceiling with 5/8" gypsum board applied parallel to the framing members.

    A. 16
    B. 19.2
    C. 24
    D. 28

Timed Exam 6 - 55. At least one egress door shall be provided for each dwelling unit. The egress door shall be side-hinged, and shall provide a minimum clear width of _____ when measured between the face of the door and the stop, with the door open 90 degrees (1.57 rad).

    A. 30 inches (762 mm)
    B. 32 inches (813 mm)
    C. 34 inches (864 mm)
    D. 36 inches (914 mm)

Timed Exam 6 - 56. When more than one smoke alarm is required to be installed within an individual dwelling unit the alarm devices shall be _____.

A. independent
B. within audible distance of each other
C. placed a uniform distances within the dwelling
D. interconnected

Timed Exam 6 - 57. The minimum width for concrete and masonry footings for a 2 story 4-inch brick veneer over light frame or 8-inch hollow concrete masonry construction dwelling where the soil load bearing value is 1500 psf is _____ inches.

A. 12
B. 16
C. 21
D. 24

Timed Exam 6 - 58. A smoke alarm shall be installed outside each separate sleeping area in the immediate vicinity of _____.

A. the garage
B. the habitable rooms
C. all areas of the dwelling
D. the bedrooms

Timed Exam 6 - 59. For interior stairs the artificial light sources shall be capable of illuminating treads and landings to levels not less than _____ foot-candles measured at the center of treads and landings. Exceptions ignored.

A. 1
B. 2
C. 6
D. 10

Timed Exam 6 - 60. A common _____ hour fire resistance rated wall is permitted for townhouses if such walls do not contain plumbing or mechanical equipment, ducts or vents in the cavity of the common wall.

A. 1/3
B. 1/2
C. 1
D. 2

Section 1 Answers

1.	A	12	Table R403.1 Minimum Width Of Concrete, Precast Or Masonry Footings
2.	C	without requiring	R102.7.1 Additions, alterations or repairs.
3.	C	5	R310.1.1 Minimum opening area. Exception
4.	C	4	R405.2.1 Base.
5.	D	1.5	R311.8.3.3 Continuity.
6.	A	existing structure	R102.7.1 Additions, alterations or repairs.
7.	B	6	R408.6 Finished grade
8.	C	site plan	R106.2 Site plan or plot plan.
9.	B	4 3/8	R312.1.3 Opening limitations. Exceptions: 2
10.	B	11	R311.7.5.3 Nosings. Exceptions:
11.	D	3.5	R506.1 General.
12.	B	3/8	R311.7.5.3 Nosings.
13.	C	ASTM D 5055	R502.1.4 Prefabricated wood I-joists.
14.	B	60 feet (18 288 mm), 3:1	R602.12.1 Circumscribed rectangle.
15.	A	16 X 24	R408.4 Access.
16.	D	B or C	R311.7.5.2 Treads.
17.	B	6	R1003.17 Masonry chimney cleanout openings
18.	D	34, 38	R311.8.3.1 Height.
19.	D	stepped	R403.1.5 Slope.
20.	C	accepted engineering practice	R602.3 Design and construction.
21.	A	keys, tools or special knowledge	R310.1.4 Operational constraints.
22.	D	40	R602.6 Drilling and notching studs. 1.
23.	C	8	R606.12.3.3 Minimum reinforcement for masonry columns.
24.	A	4 inches by 4 inches	R407.3 Structural requirements.
25.	D	shall not thereby be rendered liable personally and is hereby relieved from personal liability	R104.8 Liability.
26.	B	second floor	R505.3.6 Floor cantilevers
27.	D	all of the above	R311.7.6 Landings for stairways.
28.	A	balloon-frame	R301.1.2 Construction systems.
29.	B	2	R905.3.3.2 High slope roofs.
30.	C	foundation inspection	R109.1.1 Foundation inspection.

31.	D	3/4, 11/4	R311.7.5.3 Nosings.
32.	A	inside	R303.7.1 Light activation.
33.	C	4, 6	R404.1.6 Height above finished grade.
34.	B	1/2	R316.4 Thermal barrier.
35.	B	#4 at 48″ o.c.	Table R404.1.1(2) 8-Inch Masonry Foundation Walls With Reinforcing
36.	A	PAN FLASHING	SECTION R202 DEFINITIONS, PAN FLASHING.
37.	A	1	R802.3 Framing details.
38.	A	16	R602.3.1 Stud size, height and spacing. Exceptions
39.	A	12, 6	R1003.2 Footings and foundations.
40.	C	18 X 24	R408.4 Access.
41.	D	toenails or nails subject to withdrawal	R311.5.1 Construction Attachment.
42.	D	REVIEWED FOR CODE COMPLIANCE.	R106.3.1 Approval of construction documents.
43.	A	fees have been paid	R108.1 Payment of fees.
44.	C	180	R105.3.2 Time limitation of application.
45.	A	walkways	R303.5.2 Exhaust openings.
46.	B	200	R105.2 Work exempt from permit.
47.	C	registered design professional, registered design professional	R106.1 Submittal documents.
48.	B	7	R105.2 Work exempt from permit.
49.	C	12	R502.10 Framing of openings
50.	B	sink	R306.2 Kitchen.
51.	C	7.75	R311.7.5.1 Risers.
52.	B	5/8	Table R503.1 Minimum Thickness Of Lumber Floor Sheathing
53.	C	four times	R1003.9.3 Rain caps.
54.	A	6 feet 8 inches	R305.1 Minimum height.
55.	A	Severe	FIGURE R301.2(3) WEATHERING PROBABILITY MAP FOR CONCRETE
56.	C	demolished	R106.2 Site plan or plot plan.
57.	C	12 solid	Table R404.1.1(1) Plain Masonry Foundation Walls
58.	C	key or special knowledge or effort	R311.2 Egress door
59.	D	6 feet, 8 inches, 6 feet, 4 inches	R305.1.1 Basements. Exception
60.	B	12 feet	R311.7.3 Vertical rise.
61.	C	the permit application shall be submitted within the next working business day	R105.2.1 Emergency repairs.

62.	C	6	R505.3.6 Floor cantilevers.
63.	C	7	R305.1 Minimum height.
64.	B	18-5	Table R802.4(2) Ceiling Joist Spans For Common Lumber Species (Uninhabitable Attics With Limited Storage, Live Load = 20 Psf, L/ = 240)
65.	B	34	R312.1.1 Where required.
66.	C	3, 3	R502.6.1 Floor systems.
67.	D	3-8d	Table R602.3(1) Fastener Schedule For Structural Members. Item 2
68.	B	gypsum board	R302.7 Under-stair protection.
69.	C	6	R403.1.6 Foundation anchorage.
70.	B	1/4	R1001.5.1 Steel fireplace units.
71.	D	PHOTOVOLTAIC MODULES/SHINGLES	SECTION R202 DEFINITIONS, PHOTOVOLTAIC MODULES/SHINGLES
72.	C	8	R303.1 Habitable rooms.
73.	B	1/2-inch (12.7 mm)	R501.3 Fire protection of floors.
74.	D	does not swing over the stairs	R311.7.6 Landings for stairways. Exception:
75.	C	36	R311.7.1 Width.
76.	C	Oriented strand lumber (OSL)	SECTION R202 DEFINITIONS, Oriented strand lumber (OSL)
77.	A	2,000	Table R401.4.1 Presumptive Load Bearing Values Of Foundation Materials
78.	D	at the line of dwelling unit separation	R302.11 Fireblocking. 6.
79.	A	12	Table R403.1 Minimum Width Of Concrete, Precast Or Masonry Footings
80.	C	window well	R310.1 Emergency escape and rescue required
81.	D	40, 65	R505.2.5.2 Web hole reinforcing.
82.	C	450	R302.9.2 Smoke-developed index.
83.	C	8	R606.2.1 Minimum thickness.
84.	D	6 feet 7 inches	Table R502.5(1) Girder Spans And Header Spans For Exterior Bearing Walls (Maximum Spans For Douglas Fir-Larch, Hem-Fir, Southern Pine And Spruce-Pine-Fir And Required Number Of Jack Studs)
85.	D	All of the above	R311.8.2 Landings required.

86.	A	16 feet (4877 mm) , 48 inches (1219 mm), 16 feet (4877 mm)	R602.10.2.3 Minimum number of braced wall panels.
87.	D	9 1/2	R311.7.10.1 Spiral stairways.
88.	D	12,000	Table R401.4.1 Presumptive Load Bearing Values Of Foundation Materials
89.	B	wall or assembly	R302.2.1 Continuity.
90.	B	2	Table R502.5(2) Girder Spans And Header Spans For Interior Bearing Walls (Maximum Spans For Douglas Fir-Larch, Hem-Fir, Southern Pine And Spruce-Pine-Fir And Required Number Of Jack Studs)
91.	C	30	R302.2.2 Parapets 1.
92.	B	at least two sides	R309.2 Carports.
93.	B	4	R905.2.2 Slope.
94.	A	key	R311.2 Egress door.
95.	B	0	FIGURE R301.2(1)
96.	A	26	R311.7.10.1 Spiral stairways.
97.	B	16	Table R403.1 Minimum Width Of Concrete, Precast Or Masonry Footings
98.	C	bathtub or shower	R306.1 Toilet facilities.
99.	C	45	R403.1.7.2 Footing setback from descending slope surfaces.
100.	B	5, 7	R304.4 Height effect on room area.
101.	B	8, 24	R602.7.3 Nonbearing walls.
102.	C	1	R302.3 Two-family dwellings.
103.	B	7	R304.3 Minimum dimensions.
104.	C	.375	R311.7.5.1 Risers.
105.	D	not be limited	R316.5.2 Roofing.
106.	C	conditions of the listing and manufacturer's instructions shall apply	R102.4 Referenced codes and standards. Exception
107.	C	certificate of occupancy	R110.1 Use and occupancy.
108.	C	150	R806.2 Minimum vent area.
109.	B	most restrictive	R102.1 General.
110.	D	a registered design professional.	R502.11.3 Alterations to trusses.
111.	B	No. 4 bar	R403.1.3.2 Slabs-on-ground with turned-down footings.
112.	C A	All	R308.4.4 Glazing in guards and railings.
113.	B	Let-in-bracing	TABLE R602.10.4 BRACING METHODS

114.	C	4	R506.2.2 Base.
115.	A	2 x 12	R502.7.1 Bridging.
116.	A	approved pressure preservative treated wood suitable for ground contact use	R317.1.2 Ground contact.
117.	C	directly over each stairway section	R303.7 Stairway illumination. Exception
118.	D	12	R311.8.3 Handrails required.
119.	D	60	R602.6 Drilling and notching studs. 2.
120.	B	until approved by the building official	R111.1 Connection of service utilities.
121.	B	16	Table R403.1 Minimum Width Of Concrete, Precast Or Masonry Footings
122.	C	one-sixth	R502.8.1 Sawn lumber.
123.	A	2	R504.1.1 Unbalanced soil loads.
124.	C	12 B &S *Protest of this book* P. 167	TABLE R602.10.3(1) BRACING REQUIREMENTS BASED ON WIND SPEED
125.	B	1,000	R302.12 Draftstopping
126.	A	Any special stipulations and conditions of the building permit.	R110.3 Certificate issued.
127.	A	is authorized to examine	R105.9 Preliminary inspection.
128.	C	30	R311.7.5.1 Risers. Exceptions:
129.	B	1/2	R302.3 Two-family dwellings. Exceptions 1.
130.	C	3000	Table R402.2 Minimum Specified Compressive Strength Of Concrete
131.	A	approved private sewage disposal system	R306.3 Sewage disposal.
132.	C	18-1	Table R802.5.1(3) Rafter Spans For Common Lumber Species (Ground Snow Load=30 Psf, Ceiling Not Attached To Rafters, L/ = 180)
133.	C	4	R1003.10 Wall thickness.
134.	D	any or all of the above	R317.1.3 Geographical areas.
135.	C	26	R302.5.2 Duct penetration.
136.	A	at least the equivalent of that prescribed in this code	R104.11 Alternative materials, design and methods of construction and equipment.
137.	C	FLAME SPREAD INDEX	SECTION R202 DEFINITIONS, FLAME SPREAD INDEX

138.	D	All glazing in railings regardless of an area or height	R308.4.4 Glazing in guards and railings.
139.	D	#6 at 56" o.c.	Table R404.1.1(4) 12-Inch Masonry Foundation Walls With Reinforcing
140.	A	0.054, 8	R602.6.1 Drilling and notching of top plate.
141.	B	20	R310.1.3 Minimum opening width.
142.	A	16	Table R602.3(5) Size, Height And Spacing Of Wood Studs
143.	B	No	R309.5 Fire sprinklers.
144.	A	189	TABLE R802.11 RAFTER OR TRUSS UPLIFT CONNECTION FORCES FROM WIND (POUNDS PER CONNECTION)
145.	A	6 feet	R307.2 Bathtub and shower spaces.
146.	B	20	Table R503.2.1.1(2) Allowable Spans For Sanded Plywood Combination Subfloor Underlayment
147.	D	32	Table R503.2.1.1(1) Allowable Spans And Loads For Wood Structural Panels For Roof And Subfloor Sheathing And Combination Subfloor Underlayment
148.	A	3	R308.4.1 Glazing in doors. Exceptions 1
149.	D	such frozen condition is of a permanent character	R403.1.4.1 Frost protection.
150.	B	13/8, 13/8, 20	R302.5.1 Opening protection.
151.	A	above	R311.7.8.2 Continuity.
152.	B	SMOKE-DEVELOPED INDEX.	SECTION R202 DEFINITIONS, SMOKE-DEVELOPED INDEX
153.	B	6	R312.1.3 Opening limitations. Exceptions: 1
154.	A	10	R311.7.5.2.1 Winder treads.
155.	D	6	R303.7.1 Light activation.
156.	C	shall not be reused unless approved by the building official	R104.9.1 Used materials and equipment.
157.	A	1.5	R502.6 Bearing.
158.	D	#6 at 40" o.c.	Table R404.1.1(3) 10-Inch Foundation Walls With Reinforcing
159.	C	reasonable times	R104.6 Right of entry.
160.	D	12	Table R404.1.1(1) Plain Masonry Foundation Walls
161.	B	30	R311.7.5.1 Risers.
162.	B	10	R311.7.5.2 Treads.

163.	A	4	R303.1 Habitable rooms
164.	C	11/4, 2	R311.7.8.3 Grip-size. 1.
165.	C	one full story below the upper level	R314.3 Location. 3.
166.	C	4	R905.6.2 Deck slope.
167.	A	noncombustible	R309.1 Floor surface.
168.	D	3500	Table R402.2 Minimum Specified Compressive Strength Of Concrete
169.	A	4 feet 5 inches	Table R502.5(2) Girder Spans And Header Spans For Interior Bearing Walls (Maximum Spans For Douglas Fir-Larch, Hem-Fir, Southern Pine And Spruce-Pine-Fir And Required Number Of Jack Studs)
170.	B	8 feet 9 inches	Table R502.3.1(2) Floor Joist Spans For Common Lumber Species (Residential Living Areas, Live Load = 40 Psf
171.	C	2, 10, 3	R1003.9 Termination.
172.	C	not be allowed	R505.3.5 Cutting and notching.
173.	C	12feet 6 inches	Table R502.3.1(1) Floor Joist Spans For Common Lumber Species (Residential Sleeping Areas, Live Load = 30 Psf, L/ = 360)
174.	B	4	R502.10 Framing of openings
175.	D	fire-resistance rated	TABLE R302.1(1) EXTERIOR WALLS, It is not state whether the other structure is required or is not required to be fire resistance rated, so not enough information to answer.
176.	B	22X30	R807.1 Attic access.
177.	A	at the turn	R311.7.8.2 Continuity. Exceptions 1.
178.	A	4	R312.2.1 Window sills.
179.	C	12	R505.3.3.2 Joist bottom flange bracing/blocking.
180.	D	6, 9, 6	R606.2.1 Minimum thickness.
181.	D	lbs. per 100 sq ft	R318.2 Chemical termiticide treatment.

182.	A	5 feet 1 inches	Table R502.5(1) Girder Spans And Header Spans For Exterior Bearing Walls (Maximum Spans For Douglas Fir-Larch, Hem-Fir, Southern Pine And Spruce-Pine-Fir And Required Number Of Jack Studs)
183.	C	one-sixth, one-third, one-third	R502.8.1 Sawn lumber.
184.	A	specific	R102.1 General.
185.	C	21	Table R403.1 Minimum Width Of Concrete, Precast Or Masonry Footings
186.	C	entirely below groundwater level or continuously submerged in fresh water	R317.1.2 Ground contact.
187.	D	Only if it is heated.	R506.2.3 Vapor retarder. Exception 1 and 2.
188.	B	automatic	R313.1 Townhouse automatic fire sprinkler systems.
189.	A	6	R311.7.5.2.1 Winder treads.
190.	A	4 inches (305 mm)	R606.6.1 Pier cap.
191.	D	5/8-inch Type X gypsum board	Table R302.6 Dwelling/Garage Separation
192.	B	6'-0"	TABLE R703.7.3.1 Allowable Spans For Lintels Supporting Masonry Veneer
193.	A	24, 60	R308.4.2 Glazing adjacent doors.
194.	D	any or all of the above	R316.5.4 Crawl spaces.
195.	D	11feet 8 inches	Table R502.3.1(1) Floor Joist Spans For Common Lumber Species (Residential Sleeping Areas, Live Load = 30 Psf, L/ = 360)
196.	C	l/600	R610.5.1 Deflection.
197.	D	interconnected	R314.5 Interconnection.
198.	A	30, 30	R807.1 Attic access.
199.	C	5	R602.3.3 Bearing studs.
200.	D	No. 4	R502.1.2 Blocking and Subflooring.
201.	D	Wood structural panel	TABLE R602.10.4 BRACING METHODS
202.	A	36 inches	R311.7.6 Landings for stairways.
203.	B	two or fewer	R311.3.2 Floor elevations for other exterior doors. Exception
204.	A	safety terminals	R311.7.8.2 Continuity.
205.	C	three	R101.2 Scope.

206.	A	2500	Table R402.2 Minimum Specified Compressive Strength Of Concrete
207.	C	120	R304.1 Minimum area.
208.	B	3/4	R505.1.2 In-line framing. 1.
209.	A	25	R303.2 Adjoining rooms.
210.	B	1.5	R502.6 Bearing.
211.	C	24	Table R602.3(3) Wood Structural Panel Wall Sheathing
212.	D	C or D	Table N1102.1 Insulation And Fenestration Requirements By Component
213.	A	L/Δ = 360)	Table R502.3.1(1) Floor Joist Spans For Common Lumber Species (Residential Sleeping Areas, Live Load = 30 Psf
214.	A	1	R303.7 Stairway illumination.
215.	A	7.75	R311.3.1 Floor elevations at the required egress doors, Exception
216.	D	approximately equal areas	R302.12 Draftstopping
217.	C	a nonabsorbent surface	R307.2 Bathtub and shower spaces.
218.	B	Three	R301.2.2.3.1 Height limitations.
219.	A	12	R403.1.4 Minimum depth.
220.	A	11/2 inch (38 mm)	R602.10.10 Panel joints.
221.	A	1-1/2	R311.7.8.2 Continuity.
222.	A	1,500	Table R401.4.1 Presumptive Load Bearing Values Of Foundation Materials
223.	A	permit holder or their agent	R109.3 Inspection requests.
224.	B	32 inches (813 mm)	R311.2 Egress door.
225.	A	9/16	R311.7.5.3 Nosings.
226.	C	existing	R313.1 Townhouse automatic fire sprinkler systems. Exception:
227.	C	4 feet (1219 mm)	R602.10.1.2 Offsets along a braced wall line.
228.	D	bedrooms	R314.3 Location. 2.
229.	A	prior to installation	R502.11.4 Truss design drawings.
230.	D	Manufacturer's installation instructions	R106.1.2 Manufacturer's installation instructions.
231.	C	the building wiring	R314.4 Power source.
232.	B	1/2	R311.7.5.3 Nosings.
233.	C	1/4, 1/2	R303.6 Outside opening protection.
234.	B	1/3	R502.8.1 Sawn lumber.
235.	A	75, 450	R316.3 Surface burning characteristics.

236.	C	24	Table R503.2.1.1(1) Allowable Spans And Loads For Wood Structural Panels For Roof And Subfloor Sheathing And Combination Subfloor Underlayment
237.	B	9	R310.2 Window wells
238.	A	2	R905.2.2 Slope.
239.	A	11/2, 3	R802.6 Bearing.
240.	C	1.5	R311.3.1 Floor elevations at the required egress doors.
241.	C	11/2 inches (38 mm)	R607.3 Installation of wall ties.
242.	C	4,000	Table R401.4.1 Presumptive Load Bearing Values Of Foundation Materials
243.	B	2-percent slope	R311.7.7 Stairway walking surface.
244.	C	3	R502.6 Bearing.
245.	D	five or fewer	R101.2 Scope. Exceptions: 2.
246.	B	to the underside of the roof sheathing	R302.3 Two-family dwellings.
247.	C	Double strength glass.	R308.6.2 Permitted materials.
248.	C	3-16d	Table R602.3(1) Fastener Schedule For Structural Members. Item 6
249.	D	14'-1"	Table R505.3.2(1) Allowable Spans For Cold-Formed Steel Joists Single Spans, 33 Ksi Steel
250.	A	6 feet 6 inches	R311.7.10.1 Spiral stairways.
251.	D	A and C	R311.6 Hallways.
252.	D	1.625	Table R505.2(1) Cold-Formed Steel Joist Sizes
253.	A	11/16	Table R503.1 Minimum Thickness Of Lumber Floor Sheathing
254.	D	4.5	R311.7.1 Width.
255.	B	carbon monoxide	R315.1 Carbon monoxide alarms.
256.	B	6 inches (152 mm)	R404.1.2.3.4 Proportioning and slump of concrete.
257.	D	three, 4	R308.6.8 Curbs for skylights.
258.	B	4	R502.10 Framing of openings.
259.	C	6A	Table N1101.2 CLIMATE ZONES, MOISTURE REGIMES, AND WARM-HUMID DESIGNATIONS BY STATE, COUNTY AND TERRITORY
260.	A	I	Table R405.1 Properties Of Soils Classified According To The Unified Soil Classification System
261.	D	61/4	R311.7.8.3 Grip-size. 2

262.	D	24-0	Table R802.4(1) Ceiling Joist Spans For Common Lumber Species (Uninhabitable Attics Without Storage, Live Load = 10 Psf, L/ = 240)
263.	B	4 inches (102 mm), 1/2 inch (12.7 mm)	R319.1 Address numbers.
264.	D	6, 10	R401.3 Drainage.
265.	D	notices or orders	R104.3 Notices and orders.
266.	B	enforce compliance with the provisions of this code	R104.2 Applications and permits.
267.	D	lowest	R311.7.8.2 Continuity.
268.	B	two	R309.2 Carports.
269.	C	24	R1003.11.3 Gas appliances.
270.	B	40 inches	Table R502.3.3(2) Cantilever Spans For Floor Joists Supporting Exterior Balcony,
271.	A	are exempt	R316.5.5 Foam-filled exterior doors.
272.	A	23'- 4"	Table R505.3.2(1) Allowable Spans For Cold-Formed Steel Joists Single Spans, 33 Ksi Steel
273.	A	one openable emergency escape and rescue opening	R310.1 Emergency escape and rescue required.
274.	D	8	Table R404.1.1(1) Plain Masonry Foundation Walls
275.	C	100	Table R503.2.1.1(1) Allowable Spans And Loads For Wood Structural Panels For Roof And Subfloor Sheathing And Combination Subfloor Underlayment
276.	C	5.7	R310.1.1 Minimum opening area.
277.	A	dampproofed	R404.2.5 Drainage and dampproofing.
278.	D	42	Table R403.1 Minimum Width Of Concrete, Precast Or Masonry Footings
279.	A	2 X 2	R502.6.2 Joist framing.
280.	A	25	R602.6 Drilling and notching studs. 1.
281.	C	Fireblocking	R302.11 Fireblocking. 2.
282.	A	1	R806.3 Vent and insulation clearance.
283.	A	4	R311.7.5.1 Risers.
284.	D	on each side	R311.3 Floors and landings at exterior doors.

285.	D	4	R606.14 Beam supports.
286.	A	25, 450	R302.10.1 Insulation.
287.	D	any of the above	R310.4 Bars, grills, covers and screens.
288.	B	new work and a permit shall be obtained	R105.2 Work exempt from permit.
289.	C	60, 40, 3	R505.1.1 Applicability limits.
290.	A	3	R502.10 Framing of openings.
291.	C	four	R311.7.8 Handrails.
292.	A	3-8d	Table R602.3(1) Fastener Schedule For Structural Members , Item 1
293.	B	1/2-inch gypsum board or equivalent	Table R302.6 Dwelling/Garage Separation
294.	D	all of the above	R317.2.1 Required information.
295.	D	foundation	R301.1 Application.
296.	D	shall not be permitted	R302.5.1 Opening protection.
297.	A	1	R316.5.1 Masonry or concrete construction.
298.	C	either of the above	R317.1.4 Wood columns.
299.	B	200	TABLE R802.11 RAFTER OR TRUSS UPLIFT CONNECTION FORCES FROM WIND (POUNDS PER CONNECTION)
300.	A	6 solid or 8	Table R404.1.1(1) Plain Masonry Foundation Walls
301.	C	8	R602.10.1.4 Angled walls.
302.	C	fuel-fired appliances	R315.3 Where required in existing dwellings.
303.	B	24	R310.1.2 Minimum opening height.
304.	B	10	R403.1.5 Slope.
305.	C	25	R905.7.2 Deck slope.
306.	B	25, 450	R302.10.2 Loose-fill insulation.
307.	A	2, 24	R702.3.2 Wood framing.
308.	B	#4 at 72″ o.c.	Table R404.1.1(4) 12-Inch Masonry Foundation Walls With Reinforcing
309.	D	Plain Concrete, none	Table R404.1.2(4) Minimum Vertical Reinforcement For 10-Inch Nominal Flat Concrete Basement Walls
310.	A	0.12	R302.10.4 Exposed attic insulation.
311.	C	braced	R404.1.7 Backfill placement.
312.	B	3	R802.3.2 Ceiling joists lapped.
313.	D	1-1/2 T&G	Table R503.1 Minimum Thickness Of Lumber Floor Sheathing

314.	D	Ground-source heat pump loop systems tested in accordance with Section M2105.1	R109.1.2 Plumbing, mechanical, gas and electrical systems inspection, Exception
315.	C	60	R308.4.5 Glazing and wet surfaces.
316.	A	UL 2034	R315.4 Alarm requirements.
317.	B	2	R502.7 Lateral restraint at supports.
318.	D	400	R403.1.4.1 Frost protection. Exception 2.
319.	D	19-2	Table R802.5.1(3) Rafter Spans For Common Lumber Species (Ground Snow Load=30 Psf, Ceiling Not Attached To Rafters, L/ = 180)
320.	A	150	R408.1 Ventilation.
321.	C	50	Table R1003.14(1) Net Cross-Sectional Area Of Round Flue Sizes
322.	C	the approval of the building official.	R109.4 Approval required.
323.	A	36	R311.3 Floors and landings at exterior doors.
324.	C	NFPA 72	R314.1 Smoke detection and notification.
325.	A	such expert opinion	R104.4 Inspections.
326.	A	considered a separate building	R302.2 Townhouses.
327.	D	18	Table R602.3.1 Maximum Allowable Length Of Wood Wall Studs Exposed To Wind Speeds Of 100 Mph Or Less In Seismic Design Categories A, B, C and D0, D1 And D2
328.	B	Swings and other playground equipment.	R105.2 Work exempt from permit.
329.	C	fireblocked	R1003.19 Chimney fireblocking.
330.	B	16	R503.1.1 End joints.
331.	D	all of the above	R314.3 Location.
332.	C	60, 40	R602.6 Drilling and notching studs, Exceptions
333.	D	0.0179	Table R905.2.8.2 Valley Lining Material
334.	D	none of the above	R310.1 Emergency escape and rescue required
335.	A	3	R303.3 Bathrooms.
336.	D	shall not be cut or notched	R804.3.4 Cutting and notching.
337.	C	180, 180	R105.5 Expiration.
338.	C	minimum	R101.3 Intent.
339.	D	16, 8	R1001.10 Hearth extension dimensions.

340.	A	15/32	R316.5.2 Roofing.
341.	C	18.9 sf	R806.2 Minimum vent area. The minimum net free ventilating area shall be 1/150 of the area of the vented space.
342.	B	4	R602.9 Cripple walls.
343.	E	All of the above	R308.4.1 Glazing in doors. Exceptions 1 and 2, so it is not always.
344.	A	bottom	R407.3 Structural requirements.
345.	A	16	Table R702.3.5 Minimum Thickness And Application Of Gypsum Board
346.	C	hot-dipped galvanized steel, stainless steel, silicon bronze or copper.	R317.3.3 Fasteners for fire-retardant-treated wood used in exterior applications or wet or damp locations.
347.	E	all of the above	R105.2 Work exempt from permit.
348.	B	24	R505.3.6 Floor cantilevers
349.	B	three	SECTION R202 DEFINITIONS, BASIC WIND SPEED
350.	B	accept reports of inspection by approved agencies or individuals	R104.4 Inspections.
351.	D	any of the above	R314.3.1 Alterations, repairs and additions. Exceptions: 1.
352.	D *2 (-1 p 48*		R302.2 Townhouses. Exception
353.	D	34, 38	R311.7.8.1 Height.
354.	B	6 feet 8 inches	R311.7.2 Headroom
355.	C	3,000	Table R401.4.1 Presumptive Load Bearing Values Of Foundation Materials
356.	B	4 feet 1 inches	Table R502.5(2) Girder Spans And Header Spans For Interior Bearing Walls (Maximum Spans For Douglas Fir-Larch, Hem-Fir, Southern Pine And Spruce-Pine-Fir And Required Number Of Jack Studs)
357.	B	6, 2	R401.3 Drainage, Exception
358.	A	render interpretations	R104.1 General.
359.	A	twelve	R311.8.1 Maximum slope.
360.	D	Poorly graded sands or gravelly sands, little or no fines.	Table R405.1 Properties Of Soils Classified According To The Unified Soil Classification System
361.	D	all of the above	R311.7.5.2 Treads.

362.	D	7 feet 8 inches	Table R502.5(2) Girder Spans And Header Spans For Interior Bearing Walls (Maximum Spans For Douglas Fir-Larch, Hem-Fir, Southern Pine And Spruce-Pine-Fir And Required Number Of Jack Studs)
363.	C	thrust	R802.3.2 Ceiling joists lapped.
364.	A	location of all joints	R502.11.4 Truss design drawings.
365.	E	all of the above conditions must be present	R316.5.9 Interior trim.
366.	A	1/2 inch	R317.3.1 Fasteners for preservative-treated wood. Exception 1
367.	C	16	R408.1 Ventilation.
368.	C	permit holder or his agent	R109.1 Types of inspections.
369.	B	24	R602.3.2 Top plate.
370.	C	31.5, 27	R311.7.1 Width.
371.	B	44	R310.1 Emergency escape and rescue required
372.	A	shall not	R102.2 Other laws.
373.	A	4, 61/4, 21/4	R311.7.8.3 Grip-size.. 1.
374.	C	2,000	R316.5.7 Foam backer board.
375.	A	3-10d	Table R602.3(1) Fastener Schedule For Structural Members, Item 3
376.	C	70	R304.2 Other rooms.
377.	B	A new installation layer of roofing may sometimes be applied over the existing.	R907.3 Recovering versus replacement.
378.	C	68°F, 3, 2	R303.9 Required heating.
379.	C	0, 6	TABLE R302.1(2) EXTERIOR WALLS DWELLINGS WITH FIRE SPRINKLERS, sub note a.
380.	D	9 feet 8 inches	Table R502.3.1(1) Floor Joist Spans For Common Lumber Species (Residential Sleeping Areas, Live Load = 30 Psf, L/ = 360)
381.	A	not less than 21/4 and not more than 3 times the sum of separate volumes of lime, if used, and cement	Table R607.1 Mortar Proportions
382.	A	sloped to facilitate the movement of liquids to a drain or toward the main vehicle entry doorway	R309.1 Floor surface
383.	A	3/8	R311.7.5.2.1 Winder treads.

384.	D	12	Table R404.1.1(1) Plain Masonry Foundation Walls

Section 2 Timed Exams Answers

Timed Exam 1 - 1.	B	new work and a permit shall be obtained	R105.2 Work exempt from permit.
Timed Exam 1 - 2.	C	3000	Table R402.2 Minimum Specified Compressive Strength Of Concrete
Timed Exam 1 - 3.	C A	All	R308.4.4 Glazing in guards and railings.
Timed Exam 1 - 4.	B	6	R408.6 Finished grade
Timed Exam 1 - 5.	C	7	R305.1 Minimum height.
Timed Exam 1 - 6.	C	30	R311.7.5.1 Risers. Exceptions:
Timed Exam 1 - 7.	A	4 inches (305 mm)	R606.6.1 Pier cap.
Timed Exam 1 - 8.	D	6	R303.7.1 Light activation.
Timed Exam 1 - 9.	C	fuel-fired appliances	R315.3 Where required in existing dwellings.
Timed Exam 1 - 10.	B	20	R310.1.3 Minimum opening width.
Timed Exam 1 - 11.	C	180	R105.3.2 Time limitation of application.
Timed Exam 1 - 12.	B	7	R304.3 Minimum dimensions.
Timed Exam 1 - 13.	C	shall not be reused unless approved by the building official	R104.9.1 Used materials and equipment.
Timed Exam 1 - 14.	C D	12 solid	Table R404.1.1(1) Plain Masonry Foundation Walls
Timed Exam 1 - 15.	D	on each side	R311.3 Floors and landings at exterior doors.
Timed Exam 1 - 16.	C	3-16d	Table R602.3(1) Fastener Schedule For Structural Members. Item 6
Timed Exam 1 - 17.	C	conditions of the listing and manufacturer's instructions shall apply	R102.4 Referenced codes and standards. Exception
Timed Exam 1 - 18.	C	window well	R310.1 Emergency escape and rescue required
Timed Exam 1 - 19.	C	36	R311.7.1 Width.
Timed Exam 1 - 20.	C	accepted engineering practice	R602.3 Design and construction.
Timed Exam 1 - 21.	D	all of the above	R317.2.1 Required information.

Timed Exam 1 - 22.	A	Severe	FIGURE R301.2(3) WEATHERING PROBABILITY MAP FOR CONCRETE
Timed Exam 1 - 23.	A	prior to installation	R502.11.4 Truss design drawings.
Timed Exam 1 - 24.	C	registered design professional, registered design professional	R106.1 Submittal documents.
Timed Exam 1 - 25.	A	PAN FLASHING	SECTION R202 DEFINITIONS, PAN FLASHING.
Timed Exam 1 - 26.	C	11/2 inches (38 mm)	R607.3 Installation of wall ties.
Timed Exam 1 - 27.	C	entirely below groundwater level or continuously submerged in fresh water	R317.1.2 Ground contact.
Timed Exam 1 - 28.	A	2 x 12	R502.7.1 Bridging.
Timed Exam 1 - 29.	B D	two or fewer Two or fewer	R311.3.2 Floor elevations for other exterior doors. Exception
Timed Exam 1 - 30.	B	4 3/8	R312.1.3 Opening limitations. Exceptions: 2
Timed Exam 1 - 31.	C	6A	Table N1101.2 CLIMATE ZONES, MOISTURE REGIMES, AND WARM-HUMID DESIGNATIONS BY STATE, COUNTY AND TERRITORY
Timed Exam 1 - 32.	D	24-0	Table R802.4(1) Ceiling Joist Spans For Common Lumber Species (Uninhabitable Attics Without Storage, Live Load = 10 Psf, L/ = 240)
Timed Exam 1 - 33.	B	1,000	R302.12 Draftstopping
Timed Exam 1 - 34.	B	No. 4 bar	R403.1.3.2 Slabs-on-ground with turned-down footings.
Timed Exam 1 - 35.	D	19-2	Table R802.5.1(3) Rafter Spans For Common Lumber Species (Ground Snow Load=30 Psf, Ceiling Not Attached To Rafters, L/ = 180)
Timed Exam 1 - 36.	C	1	R302.3 Two-family dwellings.
Timed Exam 1 - 37.	B	4	R602.9 Cripple walls.
Timed Exam 1 - 38.	B	16	Table R403.1 Minimum Width Of Concrete, Precast Or Masonry Footings
Timed Exam 1 - 39.	B	1/2	R316.4 Thermal barrier.
Timed Exam 1 - 40.	B	three	SECTION R202 DEFINITIONS, BASIC WIND SPEED
Timed Exam 1 - 41.	C	3, 3	R502.6.1 Floor systems.

Timed Exam 1 - 42.	A	3	R308.4.1 Glazing in doors. Exceptions 1
Timed Exam 1 - 43.	B	24	R505.3.6 Floor cantilevers
Timed Exam 1 - 44.	D	Manufacturer's installation instructions	R106.1.2 Manufacturer's installation instructions.
Timed Exam 1 - 45.	D	34, 38	R311.8.3.1 Height.
Timed Exam 1 - 46.	C	1.5	R311.3.1 Floor elevations at the required egress doors.
Timed Exam 1 - 47.	A	render interpretations	R104.1 General.
Timed Exam 1 - 48.	B	9	R310.2 Window wells
Timed Exam 1 - 49.	A	23'- 4"	Table R505.3.2(1) Allowable Spans For Cold-Formed Steel Joists Single Spans, 33 Ksi Steel
Timed Exam 1 - 50.	A	25	R303.2 Adjoining rooms.
Timed Exam 1 - 51.	B	8, 24	R602.7.3 Nonbearing walls.
Timed Exam 1 - 52.	B	carbon monoxide	R315.1 Carbon monoxide alarms.
Timed Exam 1 - 53.	D	12,000	Table R401.4.1 Presumptive Load Bearing Values Of Foundation Materials
Timed Exam 1 - 54.	A	11/2, 3	R802.6 Bearing.
Timed Exam 1 - 55.	A	are exempt	R316.5.5 Foam-filled exterior doors.
Timed Exam 1 - 56.	D	42	Table R403.1 Minimum Width Of Concrete, Precast Or Masonry Footings
Timed Exam 1 - 57.	E	all of the above	R105.2 Work exempt from permit.
Timed Exam 1 - 58.	C	4,000	Table R401.4.1 Presumptive Load Bearing Values Of Foundation Materials
Timed Exam 1 - 59.	D	any or all of the above	R316.5.4 Crawl spaces.
Timed Exam 1 - 60.	A	36 inches	R311.7.6 Landings for stairways.
Timed Exam 2 - 1.	A	4 feet 5 inches	Table R502.5(2) Girder Spans And Header Spans For Interior Bearing Walls (Maximum Spans For Douglas Fir-Larch, Hem-Fir, Southern Pine And Spruce-Pine-Fir And Required Number Of Jack Studs)
Timed Exam 2 - 2.	B	accept reports of inspection by approved agencies or individuals	R104.4 Inspections.
Timed Exam 2 - 3.	B	200	R105.2 Work exempt from

			permit.
Timed Exam 2 - 4.	D	B or C	R311.7.5.2 Treads.
Timed Exam 2 - 5.	D	lbs. per 100 sq ft	R318.2 Chemical termiticide treatment.
Timed Exam 2 - 6.	C	4	R405.2.1 Base.
Timed Exam 2 - 7.	C	60, 40	R602.6 Drilling and notching studs, Exceptions
Timed Exam 2 - 8.	D	PHOTOVOLTAIC MODULES/SHINGLES	SECTION R202 DEFINITIONS, PHOTOVOLTAIC MODULES/SHINGLES
Timed Exam 2 - 9.	B	11	R311.7.5.3 Nosings. Exceptions:
Timed Exam 2 - 10.	C	8	R303.1 Habitable rooms.
Timed Exam 2 - 11.	A	2	R905.2.2 Slope.
Timed Exam 2 - 12.	C	four	R311.7.8 Handrails.
Timed Exam 2 - 13.	D	3-8d	Table R602.3(1) Fastener Schedule For Structural Members. Item 2
Timed Exam 2 - 14.	C	25	R905.7.2 Deck slope.
Timed Exam 2 - 15.	C	l/600	R610.5.1 Deflection.
Timed Exam 2 - 16.	D	all of the above	R314.3 Location.
Timed Exam 2 - 17.	C	hot-dipped galvanized steel, stainless steel, silicon bronze or copper.	R317.3.3 Fasteners for fire-retardant-treated wood used in exterior applications or wet or damp locations.
Timed Exam 2 - 18.	B	5, 7	R304.4 Height effect on room area.
Timed Exam 2 - 19.	B	#4 at 48" o.c.	Table R404.1.1(2) 8-Inch Masonry Foundation Walls With Reinforcing
Timed Exam 2 - 20.	A	12	R403.1.4 Minimum depth.
Timed Exam 2 - 21.	B	enforce compliance with the provisions of this code	R104.2 Applications and permits.
Timed Exam 2 - 22.	A	11/2 inch (38 mm)	R602.10.10 Panel joints.
Timed Exam 2 - 23.	A	3-8d	Table R602.3(1) Fastener Schedule For Structural Members , Item 1
Timed Exam 2 - 24.	C	directly over each stairway section	R303.7 Stairway illumination. Exception
Timed Exam 2 - 25.	C	NFPA 72	R314.1 Smoke detection and notification.
Timed Exam 2 - 26.	A	1.5	R502.6 Bearing.
Timed Exam 2 - 27.	D	shall not be permitted	R302.5.1 Opening protection.
Timed Exam 2 - 28.	C	12	TABLE R602.10.3(1) BRACING REQUIREMENTS BASED ON WIND SPEED

Timed Exam 2 - 29.	A	at the turn	R311.7.8.2 Continuity. Exceptions 1.
Timed Exam 2 - 30.	A	dampproofed	R404.2.5 Drainage and dampproofing.
Timed Exam 2 - 31.	B	4	R905.2.2 Slope.
Timed Exam 2 - 32.	C	24	Table R602.3(3) Wood Structural Panel Wall Sheathing
Timed Exam 2 - 33.	C	11/4, 2	R311.7.8.3 Grip-size. 1.
Timed Exam 2 - 34.	B	SMOKE-DEVELOPED INDEX.	SECTION R202 DEFINITIONS, SMOKE-DEVELOPED INDEX
Timed Exam 2 - 35.	C	6	R403.1.6 Foundation anchorage.
Timed Exam 2 - 36.	D	60	R602.6 Drilling and notching studs. 2.
Timed Exam 2 - 37.	C	existing	R313.1 Townhouse automatic fire sprinkler systems. Exception:
Timed Exam 2 - 38.	A	10	R311.7.5.2.1 Winder treads.
Timed Exam 2 - 39.	B	4 feet 1 inches	Table R502.5(2) Girder Spans And Header Spans For Interior Bearing Walls (Maximum Spans For Douglas Fir-Larch, Hem-Fir, Southern Pine And Spruce-Pine-Fir And Required Number Of Jack Studs)
Timed Exam 2 - 40.	A	is authorized to examine	R105.9 Preliminary inspection.
Timed Exam 2 - 41.	C	4	R506.2.2 Base.
Timed Exam 2 - 42.	A	noncombustible	R309.1 Floor surface.
Timed Exam 2 - 43.	B	1/2	R311.7.5.3 Nosings.
Timed Exam 2 - 44.	C	site plan	R106.2 Site plan or plot plan.
Timed Exam 2 - 45.	C	Oriented strand lumber (OSL)	SECTION R202 DEFINITIONS, Oriented strand lumber (OSL)
Timed Exam 2 - 46.	C	four times	R1003.9.3 Rain caps.
Timed Exam 2 - 47.	A	specific	R102.1 General.
Timed Exam 2 - 48.	D	3500	Table R402.2 Minimum Specified Compressive Strength Of Concrete
Timed Exam 2 - 49.	C	Double strength glass.	R308.6.2 Permitted materials.
Timed Exam 2 - 50.	C	5.7	R310.1.1 Minimum opening area.
Timed Exam 2 - 51.	B	wall or assembly	R302.2.1 Continuity.
Timed Exam 2 - 52.	A	75, 450	R316.3 Surface burning characteristics.
Timed Exam 2 - 53.	B	No	R309.5 Fire sprinklers.
Timed Exam 2 - 54.	B	6	R1003.17 Masonry chimney cleanout openings

Timed Exam 2 - 55.	B	16	Table R403.1 Minimum Width Of Concrete, Precast Or Masonry Footings
Timed Exam 2 - 56.	B	20	Table R503.2.1.1(2) Allowable Spans For Sanded Plywood Combination Subfloor Underlayment
Timed Exam 2 - 57.	D	fire-resistance rated	TABLE R302.1(1) EXTERIOR WALLS, It is not state whether the other structure is required or is not required to be fire resistance rated, so not enough information to answer.
Timed Exam 2 - 58.	C	150	R806.2 Minimum vent area.
Timed Exam 2 - 59.	A	keys, tools or special knowledge	R310.1.4 Operational constraints.
Timed Exam 2 - 60.	D	#6 at 40" o.c.	Table R404.1.1(3) 10-Inch Foundation Walls With Reinforcing
Timed Exam 3 - 1.	B	8 feet 9 inches	Table R502.3.1(2) Floor Joist Spans For Common Lumber Species (Residential Living Areas, Live Load = 40 Psf
Timed Exam 3 - 2.	D	8	Table R404.1.1(1) Plain Masonry Foundation Walls
Timed Exam 3 - 3.	A	I	Table R405.1 Properties Of Soils Classified According To The Unified Soil Classification System
Timed Exam 3 - 4.	B	22X30	R807.1 Attic access.
Timed Exam 3 - 5.	D	3.5	R506.1 General.
Timed Exam 3 - 6.	A	0.054, 8	R602.6.1 Drilling and notching of top plate.
Timed Exam 3 - 7.	A	1-1/2	R311.7.8.2 Continuity.
Timed Exam 3 - 8.	B	12 feet	R311.7.3 Vertical rise.
Timed Exam 3 - 9.	B	24	R310.1.2 Minimum opening height.
Timed Exam 3 - 10.	D	No. 4	R502.1.2 Blocking and Subflooring.
Timed Exam 3 - 11.	D	12	R311.8.3 Handrails required.
Timed Exam 3 - 12.	C	one-sixth	R502.8.1 Sawn lumber.
Timed Exam 3 - 13.	C	180, 180	R105.5 Expiration.
Timed Exam 3 - 14.	B	4	R502.10 Framing of openings
Timed Exam 3 - 15.	C	8	R602.10.1.4 Angled walls.
Timed Exam 3 - 16.	B	1.5	R502.6 Bearing.

Timed Exam 3 - 17.	D	approximately equal areas	R302.12 Draftstopping
Timed Exam 3 - 18.	E	All of the above	R308.4.1 Glazing in doors. Exceptions 1 and 2, so it is not always.
Timed Exam 3 - 19.	C	the approval of the building official.	R109.4 Approval required.
Timed Exam 3 - 20.	C	one full story below the upper level	R314.3 Location. 3.
Timed Exam 3 - 21.	C	certificate of occupancy	R110.1 Use and occupancy.
Timed Exam 3 - 22.	B	two	R309.2 Carports.
Timed Exam 3 - 23.	B	5/8	Table R503.1 Minimum Thickness Of Lumber Floor Sheathing
Timed Exam 3 - 24.	D	Only if it is heated.	R506.2.3 Vapor retarder. Exception 1 and 2.
Timed Exam 3 - 25.	A	15/32	R316.5.2 Roofing.
Timed Exam 3 - 26.	A	4	R312.2.1 Window sills.
Timed Exam 3 - 27.	A	1	R806.3 Vent and insulation clearance.
Timed Exam 3 - 28.	A	150	R408.1 Ventilation.
Timed Exam 3 - 29.	B	1/2	R302.3 Two-family dwellings. Exceptions 1.
Timed Exam 3 - 30.	A	12	Table R403.1 Minimum Width Of Concrete, Precast Or Masonry Footings
Timed Exam 3 - 31.	A	above	R311.7.8.2 Continuity.
Timed Exam 3 - 32.	D	All of the above	R311.8.2 Landings required.
Timed Exam 3 - 33.	B	6 feet 8 inches	R311.7.2 Headroom
Timed Exam 3 - 34.	D	shall not be cut or notched	R804.3.4 Cutting and notching.
Timed Exam 3 - 35.	A	16	R602.3.1 Stud size, height and spacing. Exceptions
Timed Exam 3 - 36.	C	braced	R404.1.7 Backfill placement.
Timed Exam 3 - 37.	C	7.75	R311.7.5.1 Risers.
Timed Exam 3 - 38.	B	7	R105.2 Work exempt from permit.
Timed Exam 3 - 39.	D	32	Table R503.2.1.1(1) Allowable Spans And Loads For Wood Structural Panels For Roof And Subfloor Sheathing And Combination Subfloor Underlayment
Timed Exam 3 - 40.	A	2,000	Table R401.4.1 Presumptive Load Bearing Values Of Foundation Materials
Timed Exam 3 - 41.	A	one openable emergency escape and rescue opening	R310.1 Emergency escape and rescue required.

Timed Exam 3 - 42.	B	25, 450	R302.10.2 Loose-fill insulation.
Timed Exam 3 - 43.	A	approved private sewage disposal system	R306.3 Sewage disposal.
Timed Exam 3 - 44.	A	UL 2034	R315.4 Alarm requirements.
Timed Exam 3 - 45.	D	1.625	Table R505.2(1) Cold-Formed Steel Joist Sizes
Timed Exam 3 - 46.	D	#6 at 56" o.c.	Table R404.1.1(4) 12-Inch Masonry Foundation Walls With Reinforcing
Timed Exam 3 - 47.	C	1/4, 1/2	R303.6 Outside opening protection.
Timed Exam 3 - 48.	D	such frozen condition is of a permanent character	R403.1.4.1 Frost protection.
Timed Exam 3 - 49.	A	16 X 24	R408.4 Access.
Timed Exam 3 - 50.	A	such expert opinion	R104.4 Inspections.
Timed Exam 3 - 51.	D	16, 8	R1001.10 Hearth extension dimensions.
Timed Exam 3 - 52.	B	0	FIGURE R301.2(1)
Timed Exam 3 - 53.	C	18.9 sf	R806.2 Minimum vent area. The minimum net free ventilating area shall be 1/150 of the area of the vented space.
Timed Exam 3 - 54.	D	notices or orders	R104.3 Notices and orders.
Timed Exam 3 - 55.	D	3/4, 11/4	R311.7.5.3 Nosings.
Timed Exam 3 - 56.	C	5	R310.1.1 Minimum opening area. Exception
Timed Exam 3 - 57.	A	approved pressure preservative treated wood suitable for ground contact use	R317.1.2 Ground contact.
Timed Exam 3 - 58.	D	4	R606.14 Beam supports.
Timed Exam 3 - 59.	B	4	R502.10 Framing of openings.
Timed Exam 3 - 60.	D	REVIEWED FOR CODE COMPLIANCE.	R106.3.1 Approval of construction documents.
Timed Exam 4 - 1.	C	key or special knowledge or effort	R311.2 Egress door
Timed Exam 4 - 2.	D	11feet 8 inches	Table R502.3.1(1) Floor Joist Spans For Common Lumber Species (Residential Sleeping Areas, Live Load = 30 Psf, L/ = 360)
Timed Exam 4 - 3.	C	FLAME SPREAD INDEX	SECTION R202 DEFINITIONS, FLAME SPREAD INDEX
Timed Exam 4 - 4.	D	1-1/2 T&G	Table R503.1 Minimum Thickness Of Lumber Floor

			Sheathing
Timed Exam 4 - 5.	A	existing structure	R102.7.1 Additions, alterations or repairs.
Timed Exam 4 - 6.	C	4	R1003.10 Wall thickness.
Timed Exam 4 - 7.	A	26	R311.7.10.1 Spiral stairways.
Timed Exam 4 - 8.	C	12feet 6 inches	Table R502.3.1(1) Floor Joist Spans For Common Lumber Species (Residential Sleeping Areas, Live Load = 30 Psf, L/ = 360)
Timed Exam 4 - 9.	D	foundation	R301.1 Application.
Timed Exam 4 - 10.	C	60	R308.4.5 Glazing and wet surfaces.
Timed Exam 4 - 11.	D	14'-1"	Table R505.3.2(1) Allowable Spans For Cold-Formed Steel Joists Single Spans, 33 Ksi Steel
Timed Exam 4 - 12.	D	6, 10	R401.3 Drainage.
Timed Exam 4 - 13.	A	fees have been paid	R108.1 Payment of fees.
Timed Exam 4 - 14.	A	at least the equivalent of that prescribed in this code	R104.11 Alternative materials, design and methods of construction and equipment.
Timed Exam 4 - 15.	C	foundation inspection	R109.1.1 Foundation inspection.
Timed Exam 4 - 16.	A	safety terminals	R311.7.8.2 Continuity.
Timed Exam 4 - 17.	C	6	R505.3.6 Floor cantilevers.
Timed Exam 4 - 18.	A	4 inches by 4 inches	R407.3 Structural requirements.
Timed Exam 4 - 19.	B	30	R311.7.5.1 Risers.
Timed Exam 4 - 20.	A	16 feet (4877 mm) , 48 inches (1219 mm), 16 feet (4877 mm)	R602.10.2.3 Minimum number of braced wall panels.
Timed Exam 4 - 21.	B	#4 at 72" o.c.	Table R404.1.1(4) 12-Inch Masonry Foundation Walls With Reinforcing
Timed Exam 4 - 22.	B	sink	R306.2 Kitchen.
Timed Exam 4 - 23.	A	balloon-frame	R301.1.2 Construction systems.
Timed Exam 4 - 24.	C	5	R602.3.3 Bearing studs.
Timed Exam 4 - 25.	A	2500	Table R402.2 Minimum Specified Compressive Strength Of Concrete
Timed Exam 4 - 26.	D	6 feet 7 inches	Table R502.5(1) Girder Spans And Header Spans For Exterior Bearing Walls (Maximum Spans For Douglas Fir-Larch, Hem-Fir, Southern Pine And Spruce-Pine-Fir And Required Number Of Jack Studs)

Timed Exam 4 - 27.	A	16	Table R602.3(5) Size, Height And Spacing Of Wood Studs
Timed Exam 4 - 28.	B	1/3	R502.8.1 Sawn lumber.
Timed Exam 4 - 29.	D	6 feet, 8 inches, 6 feet, 4 inches	R305.1.1 Basements. Exception
Timed Exam 4 - 30.	A	9/16	R311.7.5.3 Nosings.
Timed Exam 4 - 31.	D	Wood structural panel	TABLE R602.10.4 BRACING METHODS
Timed Exam 4 - 32.	A	36	R311.3 Floors and landings at exterior doors.
Timed Exam 4 - 33.	C	.375	R311.7.5.1 Risers.
Timed Exam 4 - 34.	A	30, 30	R807.1 Attic access.
Timed Exam 4 - 35.	C	bathtub or shower	R306.1 Toilet facilities.
Timed Exam 4 - 36.	C	45	R403.1.7.2 Footing setback from descending slope surfaces.
Timed Exam 4 - 37.	D	61/4	R311.7.8.3 Grip-size. 2
Timed Exam 4 - 38.	D	34, 38	R311.7.8.1 Height.
Timed Exam 4 - 39.	D	0.0179	Table R905.2.8.2 Valley Lining Material
Timed Exam 4 - 40.	D	40, 65	R505.2.5.2 Web hole reinforcing.
Timed Exam 4 - 41.	A	permit holder or their agent	R109.3 Inspection requests.
Timed Exam 4 - 42.	A	1	R802.3 Framing details.
Timed Exam 4 - 43.	B	until approved by the building official	R111.1 Connection of service utilities.
Timed Exam 4 - 44.	B	1/2-inch gypsum board or equivalent	Table R302.6 Dwelling/Garage Separation
Timed Exam 4 - 45.	C	30	R302.2.2 Parapets 1.
Timed Exam 4 - 46.	C	24	Table R503.2.1.1(1) Allowable Spans And Loads For Wood Structural Panels For Roof And Subfloor Sheathing And Combination Subfloor Underlayment
Timed Exam 4 - 47.	B	34	R312.1.1 Where required.
Timed Exam 4 - 48.	B	6'-0"	TABLE R703.7.3.1 Allowable Spans For Lintels Supporting Masonry Veneer
Timed Exam 4 - 49.	A	twelve	R311.8.1 Maximum slope.
Timed Exam 4 - 50.	C	4 feet (1219 mm)	R602.10.1.2 Offsets along a braced wall line.
Timed Exam 4 - 51.	A	12, 6	R1003.2 Footings and foundations.
Timed Exam 4 - 52.	A	6 feet 6 inches	R311.7.10.1 Spiral stairways.
Timed Exam 4 - 53.	C	18 X 24	R408.4 Access.
Timed Exam 4 - 54.	D	6, 9, 6	R606.2.1 Minimum thickness.
Timed Exam 4 - 55.	C	minimum	R101.3 Intent.

Timed Exam 4 - 56.	A	2 X 2	R502.6.2 Joist framing.
Timed Exam 4 - 57.	C	reasonable times	R104.6 Right of entry.
Timed Exam 4 - 58.	B	60 feet (18 288 mm), 3:1	R602.12.1 Circumscribed rectangle.
Timed Exam 4 - 59.	A	189	TABLE R802.11 RAFTER OR TRUSS UPLIFT CONNECTION FORCES FROM WIND (POUNDS PER CONNECTION)
Timed Exam 4 - 60.	A	inside	R303.7.1 Light activation.
Timed Exam 5 - 1.	A	1,500	Table R401.4.1 Presumptive Load Bearing Values Of Foundation Materials
Timed Exam 5 - 2.	A B	5 feet 1 inches *6' 4" P 121*	Table R502.5(1) Girder Spans And Header Spans For Exterior Bearing Walls (Maximum Spans For Douglas Fir-Larch, Hem-Fir, Southern Pine And Spruce-Pine-Fir And Required Number Of Jack Studs)
Timed Exam 5 - 3.	B	6	R312.1.3 Opening limitations. Exceptions: 1
Timed Exam 5 - 4.	C	either of the above	R317.1.4 Wood columns.
Timed Exam 5 - 5.	B	gypsum board	R302.7 Under-stair protection.
Timed Exam 5 - 6.	B	Swings and other playground equipment.	R105.2 Work exempt from permit.
Timed Exam 5 - 7.	A	0.12	R302.10.4 Exposed attic insulation.
Timed Exam 5 - 8.	B	10	R403.1.5 Slope.
Timed Exam 5 - 9.	C	fireblocked	R1003.19 Chimney fireblocking.
Timed Exam 5 - 10.	C	one-sixth, one-third, one-third	R502.8.1 Sawn lumber.
Timed Exam 5 - 11.	B	second floor	R505.3.6 Floor cantilevers
Timed Exam 5 - 12.	A	3	R303.3 Bathrooms.
Timed Exam 5 - 13.	D	9 1/2	R311.7.10.1 Spiral stairways.
Timed Exam 5 - 14.	D	five or fewer	R101.2 Scope. Exceptions: 2.
Timed Exam 5 - 15.	D	A and C	R311.6 Hallways.
Timed Exam 5 - 16.	B	1/2-inch (12.7 mm)	R501.3 Fire protection of floors.
Timed Exam 5 - 17.	C	18-1	Table R802.5.1(3) Rafter Spans For Common Lumber Species (Ground Snow Load=30 Psf, Ceiling Not Attached To Rafters, L/ = 180)
Timed Exam 5 - 18.	D	any of the above	R310.4 Bars, grills, covers and screens.
Timed Exam 5 - 19.	C	26	R302.5.2 Duct penetration.

Timed Exam 5 - 20.	A	25	R602.6 Drilling and notching studs. 1.
Timed Exam 5 - 21.	A	considered a separate building	R302.2 Townhouses.
Timed Exam 5 - 22.	B	2	R502.7 Lateral restraint at supports.
Timed Exam 5 - 23.	B	to the underside of the roof sheathing	R302.3 Two-family dwellings.
Timed Exam 5 - 24.	C	60, 40, 3	R505.1.1 Applicability limits.
Timed Exam 5 - 25.	C	8	R606.2.1 Minimum thickness.
Timed Exam 5 - 26.	A	key	R311.2 Egress door.
Timed Exam 5 - 27.	D	lowest	R311.7.8.2 Continuity.
Timed Exam 5 - 28.	B	4 inches (102 mm), 1/2 inch (12.7 mm)	R319.1 Address numbers.
Timed Exam 5 - 29.	D	shall not thereby be rendered liable personally and is hereby relieved from personal liability	R104.8 Liability.
Timed Exam 5 - 30.	C	12	R505.3.3.2 Joist bottom flange bracing/blocking.
Timed Exam 5 - 31.	C	not be allowed	R505.3.5 Cutting and notching.
Timed Exam 5 - 32.	C	24	R1003.11.3 Gas appliances.
Timed Exam 5 - 33.	A	3	R502.10 Framing of openings.
Timed Exam 5 - 34.	A	6 solid or 8	Table R404.1.1(1) Plain Masonry Foundation Walls
Timed Exam 5 - 35.	B	Let-in-bracing	TABLE R602.10.4 BRACING METHODS
Timed Exam 5 - 36.	A	4	R311.7.5.1 Risers.
Timed Exam 5 - 37.	C	three	R101.2 Scope.
Timed Exam 5 - 38.	B	1/4	R1001.5.1 Steel fireplace units.
Timed Exam 5 - 39.	A	6 feet 8 inches	R305.1 Minimum height.
Timed Exam 5 - 40.	C	3	R502.6 Bearing.
Timed Exam 5 - 41.	A	6	R311.7.5.2.1 Winder treads.
Timed Exam 5 - 42.	B E	C or D	Table N1102.1 Insulation And Fenestration Requirements By Component
Timed Exam 5 - 43.	A	bottom	R407.3 Structural requirements.
Timed Exam 5 - 44.	B	6, 2	R401.3 Drainage, Exception
Timed Exam 5 - 45.	B	6 inches (152 mm)	R404.1.2.3.4 Proportioning and slump of concrete.
Timed Exam 5 - 46.	A	25, 450	R302.10.1 Insulation.
Timed Exam 5 - 47.	D	4.5	R311.7.1Width.
Timed Exam 5 - 48.	B	2	R905.3.3.2 High slope roofs.
Timed Exam 5 - 49.	A	12	Table R403.1 Minimum Width Of Concrete, Precast Or Masonry Footings

Timed Exam 5 - 50.	C	2, 10, 3	R1003.9 Termination.
Timed Exam 5 - 51.	B	2	Table R502.5(2) Girder Spans And Header Spans For Interior Bearing Walls (Maximum Spans For Douglas Fir-Larch, Hem-Fir, Southern Pine And Spruce-Pine-Fir And Required Number Of Jack Studs)
Timed Exam 5 - 52.	B	at least two sides	R309.2 Carports.
Timed Exam 5 - 53.	C	8	R606.12.3.3 Minimum reinforcement for masonry columns.
Timed Exam 5 - 54.	B	40 inches	Table R502.3.3(2) Cantilever Spans For Floor Joists Supporting Exterior Balcony,
Timed Exam 5 - 55.	B	200	TABLE R802.11 RAFTER OR TRUSS UPLIFT CONNECTION FORCES FROM WIND (POUNDS PER CONNECTION)
Timed Exam 5 - 56.	D	Ground-source heat pump loop systems tested in accordance with Section M2105.1	R109.1.2 Plumbing, mechanical, gas and electrical systems inspection, Exception
Timed Exam 5 - 57.	A	Any special stipulations and conditions of the building permit.	R110.3 Certificate issued.
Timed Exam 5 - 58.	C	the permit application shall be submitted within the next working business day	R105.2.1 Emergency repairs.
Timed Exam 5 - 59.	C	4, 6	R404.1.6 Height above finished grade.
Timed Exam 5 - 60.	A	$L/\Delta = 360$)	Table R502.3.1(1) Floor Joist Spans For Common Lumber Species (Residential Sleeping Areas, Live Load = 30 Psf
Timed Exam 6 - 1.	D	All glazing in railings regardless of an area or height	R308.4.4 Glazing in guards and railings.
Timed Exam 6 - 2.	C	4	R905.6.2 Deck slope.
Timed Exam 6 - 3.	D	Plain Concrete, none	Table R404.1.2(4) Minimum Vertical Reinforcement For 10-Inch Nominal Flat Concrete Basement Walls

Timed Exam 6 - 4.	C	3,000	Table R401.4.1 Presumptive Load Bearing Values Of Foundation Materials
Timed Exam 6 - 5.	B	Three	R301.2.2.3.1 Height limitations.
Timed Exam 6 - 6.	B	18-5	Table R802.4(2) Ceiling Joist Spans For Common Lumber Species (Uninhabitable Attics With Limited Storage, Live Load = 20 Psf, L/ = 240)
Timed Exam 6 - 7.	D	stepped	R403.1.5 Slope.
Timed Exam 6 - 8.	A	1	R316.5.1 Masonry or concrete construction.
Timed Exam 6 - 9.	C	450	R302.9.2 Smoke-developed index.
Timed Exam 6 - 10.	C	demolished	R106.2 Site plan or plot plan.
Timed Exam 6 - 11.	A	walkways	R303.5.2 Exhaust openings.
Timed Exam 6 - 12.	B	2-percent slope	R311.7.7 Stairway walking surface.
Timed Exam 6 - 13.	D	5/8-inch Type X gypsum board	Table R302.6 Dwelling/Garage Separation
Timed Exam 6 - 14.	B	16	R503.1.1 End joints.
Timed Exam 6 - 15.	B	automatic	R313.1 Townhouse automatic fire sprinkler systems.
Timed Exam 6 - 16.	C	100	Table R503.2.1.1(1) Allowable Spans And Loads For Wood Structural Panels For Roof And Subfloor Sheathing And Combination Subfloor Underlayment
Timed Exam 6 - 17.	D	Poorly graded sands or gravelly sands, little or no fines.	Table R405.1 Properties Of Soils Classified According To The Unified Soil Classification System
Timed Exam 6 - 18.	D	12	Table R404.1.1(1) Plain Masonry Foundation Walls
Timed Exam 6 - 19.	B	3/8	R311.7.5.3 Nosings.
Timed Exam 6 - 20.	C	a nonabsorbent surface	R307.2 Bathtub and shower spaces.
Timed Exam 6 - 21.	D	all of the above	R311.7.6 Landings for stairways.
Timed Exam 6 - 22.	D	three, 4	R308.6.8 Curbs for skylights.
Timed Exam 6 - 23.	D	at the line of dwelling unit separation	R302.11 Fireblocking. 6.
Timed Exam 6 - 24.	A	6 feet	R307.2 Bathtub and shower spaces.
Timed Exam 6 - 25.	D	any of the above	R314.3.1 Alterations, repairs and additions. Exceptions: 1.
Timed Exam 6 - 26.	C	without requiring	R102.7.1 Additions, alterations or repairs.

Timed Exam 6 - 27.	D	any or all of the above	R317.1.3 Geographical areas.
Timed Exam 6 - 28.	D	18	Table R602.3.1 Maximum Allowable Length Of Wood Wall Studs Exposed To Wind Speeds Of 100 Mph Or Less In Seismic Design Categories A, B, C and D0, D1 And D2
Timed Exam 6 - 29.	C	the building wiring	R314.4 Power source.
Timed Exam 6 - 30.	B	3/4	R505.1.2 In-line framing. 1.
Timed Exam 6 - 31.	C	120	R304.1 Minimum area.
Timed Exam 6 - 32.	C	12	R502.10 Framing of openings
Timed Exam 6 - 33.	A	24, 60	R308.4.2 Glazing adjacent doors.
Timed Exam 6 - 34.	A	2, 24	R702.3.2 Wood framing.
Timed Exam 6 - 35.	D	400	R403.1.4.1 Frost protection. Exception 2.
Timed Exam 6 - 36.	A D	7.75 P 59	R311.3.1 Floor elevations at the required egress doors, Exception
Timed Exam 6 - 37.	D	not be limited	R316.5.2 Roofing.
Timed Exam 6 - 38.	A	4	R303.1 Habitable rooms
Timed Exam 6 - 39.	B	3	R802.3.2 Ceiling joists lapped.
Timed Exam 6 - 40.	D	a registered design professional.	R502.11.3 Alterations to trusses.
Timed Exam 6 - 41.	A	2	R504.1.1 Unbalanced soil loads.
Timed Exam 6 - 42.	A	11/16	Table R503.1 Minimum Thickness Of Lumber Floor Sheathing
Timed Exam 6 - 43.	D	toenails or nails subject to withdrawal	R311.5.1 Construction Attachment.
Timed Exam 6 - 44.	D	none of the above	R310.1 Emergency escape and rescue required
Timed Exam 6 - 45.	B	13/8, 13/8, 20	R302.5.1 Opening protection.
Timed Exam 6 - 46.	B	10	R311.7.5.2 Treads.
Timed Exam 6 - 47.	D	does not swing over the stairs	R311.7.6 Landings for stairways. Exception:
Timed Exam 6 - 48.	D	40	R602.6 Drilling and notching studs. 1.
Timed Exam 6 - 49.	C	Fireblocking	R302.11 Fireblocking. 2.
Timed Exam 6 - 50.	B	most restrictive	R102.1 General.
Timed Exam 6 - 51.	C	ASTM D 5055	R502.1.4 Prefabricated wood I-joists.
Timed Exam 6 - 52.	D	1.5	R311.8.3.3 Continuity.
Timed Exam 6 - 53.	C	50	Table R1003.14(1) Net Cross-Sectional Area Of Round Flue Sizes
Timed Exam 6 - 54.	A	16	Table R702.3.5 Minimum Thickness And Application Of

			Gypsum Board
Timed Exam 6 - 55.	B	32 inches (813 mm)	R311.2 Egress door.
Timed Exam 6 - 56.	D	interconnected	R314.5 Interconnection.
Timed Exam 6 - 57.	C	21	Table R403.1 Minimum Width Of Concrete, Precast Or Masonry Footings
Timed Exam 6 - 58.	D	bedrooms	R314.3 Location. 2.
Timed Exam 6 - 59.	A	1	R303.7 Stairway illumination.
Timed Exam 6 - 60.	D	2	R302.2 Townhouses. Exception